We are all on a journey in this life, and we each have a story to tell. Our stories include everything, whether it is good, bad or ugly. When we engage with one another, we learn how to walk in each other's shoes. The testimonies we hear give us power to do the same things with the same results. I know Jason's story. I have a similar journey. I appreciate anyone who can turn pain into a radical process of becoming like Jesus.

It is in the valley that our lives are truly adjusted to the pleasures of God. On the mountain we have sovereign encounters with majesty and beauty, and then we must return to the scene of the devastation and begin to plant what God has sowed into us. This is where we encounter the incomparable delight of the Comforter, who steps into our devastation with His own gracious touch and renovates us from the inside out.

Forgiveness that is etched in grace creates a lifestyle of loving that is powerful, releasing and effective. All who read this book will be changed, because they will be drawn into the story of Jesus walking with beauty in the fields of pain.

Graham Cooke
Author, Speaker and Publisher

No matter how much you've needed to forgive, this story will challenge you to forgive even more. Here is an astounding retelling of God's empowering forgiveness. If you find most books on forgiveness theoretical and legalistic (as I do), this book will stir you to actively walk in the very forgiveness of God. Only the Holy Spirit can bring about this kind of story!

Steve Sjogren
Church Planter and Pastor
Author of *Conspiracy of Kindness*

THE SUPERNATURAL POWER OF *Forgiveness*

It's one thing to read a moving story of betrayal, forgiveness and recovery, but quite another to watch it unfold before your eyes. Such is the role I've had with the Vallotton family since the day their world collapsed. This great family got just what they didn't deserve. The unbelievable pain was paralyzing. Yet turn after turn, they moved redemptively and discovered God's goodness in a new way. *The Supernatural Power of Forgiveness* gives us exactly what we need: honesty, inspiration and insight to enable us to understand the process to health and recovery. Both Jason and Kris have an unusual gift to communicate through writing. This is a much-needed book in the library of every believer.

Bill Johnson
Senior Leader of Bethel Church
Redding, California

Jason Vallotton, along with his father, Kris Vallotton, are laying the foundation to incredible freedom and joy in their book *The Supernatural Power of Forgiveness*. This book is unashamedly honest and challenges you to look at your own heart with the same honesty. We completely believe this book will set the captives free and heal the brokenhearted! It not only teaches you how to forgive but also how to walk it out and see it through to completion in your life. *The Supernatural Power of Forgiveness* will bring greater intimacy with the Father to every heart that embraces it.

Kim Walker-Smith and Skyler Smith
Jesus Culture

In *The Supernatural Power of Forgiveness,* Jason vulnerably exposes his story of devastating betrayal and how he wrestled for true forgiveness. This book holds the potential for the Great Comforter to come and release you from the agonizing pain that you have buried inside your own heart and bring you to a place of joy and destiny in which you actually reap a harvest in the area the enemy endeavored to destroy. I want to honor this man of God for his transparency before the body of Christ, which will serve to lead readers into a place of true freedom.

Ché Ahn

Senior Pastor, HROCK Church, Pasadena, California
President, Harvest International Ministry
International Chancellor, Wagner Leadership Institute

Through a moving story of experiencing a personal betrayal in a marriage, Kris and Jason Vallotton show how God can enable us to move beyond the hurt and desire for revenge to attain real emotional freedom and a reconciliation with those who have wronged us.

David Aikman

Bestselling Author of *Jesus in Beijing*
Former *TIME* Magazine Journalist

The Supernatural Power of Forgiveness is much more than a set of principles, a fresh Bible study or even a powerful testimony. This book is a piece of the Vallotton family's heart. In a beautiful context and style, Kris and Jason pen some of the most painful experiences of their lives. The unique approach of this book on forgiveness is the paradigm in which they lived the unfolding events. I encourage anyone seeking to learn a supernatural response to betrayal, offense or broken relationships to read this book and be forever changed.

Danny Silk

Author of *Culture of Honor* and *Loving Our Kids on Purpose*

THE SUPERNATURAL
POWER OF FORGIVENESS

THE
SUPERNATURAL
POWER

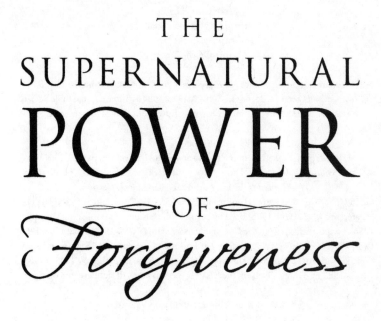

OF

Forgiveness

KRIS & JASON
VALLOTTON

Regal

From Gospel Light
Ventura, California, U.S.A.

Published by Regal
From Gospel Light
Ventura, California, U.S.A.
www.regalbooks.com
Printed in the U.S.A.

Library of Congress Cataloging-in-Publication Data
Vallotton, Kris.
The supernatural power of forgiveness : discover how to escape your prison of
pain and unlock a life of freedom / Kris Vallotton, Jason Vallotton.
p. cm.
Includes bibliographical references and index.
ISBN 978-0-8307-5737-4 (trade paper : alk. paper)
1. Forgiveness—Religious aspects—Christianity. 2. Vallotton, Kris. 3. Vallotton,
Jason. I. Vallotton, Jason. II. Title.
BV4647.F55V35 2011
241'.4—dc22
2011002931

Rights for publishing this book outside the U.S.A. or in non-English languages are
administered by Gospel Light Worldwide, an international not-for-profit ministry.
For additional information, please visit www.glww.org, email info@glww.org, or write
to Gospel Light Worldwide, 1957 Eastman Avenue, Ventura, CA 93003, U.S.A.

To order copies of this book and other Regal products in bulk quantities,
please contact us at 1-800-446-7735.

Dedication

I (Jason) dedicate this book to my loving children. The reality that
each of you has been handed has been more than grieving
to my heart. And though I have given my all to protect
you from the carnality of this world, I somehow know that you
will advance from these turbulent places, far beyond where I
could have ever launched you.

John Adams said that "people and nations are forged in the
fires of adversity," and there are no truer words in my life than these.
You kids are the jewels of my heart, and you were most often the
reason why I stayed the course during the toughest of times. I pray
that someday my life's work and convictions will make
your greatest dreams possible. As a father, I couldn't be more
proud of any children. You each have weathered the storms and
have become amazing representations of God's masterpiece.

I love you with all of me . . .
Dad

Contents

Foreword

This book is a powerful key to unlock the hearts of those who have been trapped by the pain and memories of their past traumas and experiences. Jason's vulnerable testimony will help those who have been hurt and betrayed to find courage and strength to face their own pain. His journey of love and forgiveness testifies that there is no situation beyond the unending reach of God's love and redemption. God promises us that if we give Him the ashes of our lives, He will exchange them for His beauty, no matter how big our ash heap seems to be!

Jason and Kris have shared deep insights from the heart of God that are crucial for the journey from pain into the beauty of His restoration. They have done an amazing job of writing about a difficult subject in a very transparent and moving way. Their openness and vulnerability will pave the way for many to come out of the prison of unforgiveness and in to a place of healing and freedom.

During the last 16 years of being a missionary in one of the poorest nations in the world, I have seen some of the greatest suffering imaginable. I have also had the joy of seeing God bring about restoration in the most remarkable ways! This hinges on one of the biggest decisions that we can ever make: the decision to forgive. Forgiveness makes the difference between continued torment and suffering and freedom and redemption beyond our wildest dreams.

Often, I have witnessed how those who have experienced unimaginable atrocities have come into a radical transformation beyond what they could have ever hoped for. This happened as they courageously chose to forgive. One such person is Luis. He is one of my greatest heroes. He taught me about the power of forgiveness and mercy.

I found Luis on the streets. He was sick and full of anger because he had been burned in his house (which was a cardboard box) by people who had previously been his friends. They had poured gasoline on it, tied him to the cardboard and lit it on fire, leaving him to die. He was terribly burned and had spent many months in a dilapidated local hospital. He was unhappy and bitter about being treated so horribly. His misery had brought him to a place of great brokenness, and he had nothing left to take pride in. He would often wet himself, and he lived in filth.

When I met Luis, I held him in my arms and told him about Jesus' passionate love. I invited him to come home and live with us. At the time, Luis was not very merciful or forgiving; he made his living by hitting, stealing and knifing people! But I kept telling Luis about this man named Jesus who had given up His home and riches and walked the streets—the One who left heaven and came to earth to find him. Eventually, Luis said, "I must know this man!"

One day, Luis came to me and said that he wanted to go to the streets with me so that he could tell the guys who tried to kill him that he forgave them. I watched Luis pour out extravagant mercy on many in the streets of Maputo, and I watched the favor of God increase in his broken little life.

One of our churches at that time was an unconventional congregation. We met in a brothel to reach the prostitutes. We worshipped Jesus, prayed and simply loved the resident prostitute girls. However, we weren't seeing a lot of breakthrough in the girls escaping the cycle of their destructive lifestyles. (Some of these girls were as young as 10, 11 and 12 years old, and they were selling their bodies on the streets for a bottle of Coke.) I was desperate for Jesus to set them free.

While I was on a 40-day fast (and feeling very hungry and desperate), I cried out to God to change the situation. Shortly after this, the girls fell on their knees during worship and started screaming, "We cannot sell ourselves anymore!" I started weeping for joy and asked Jesus what I should do next. I knew that I could not move these girls into the same center as the boys and that I needed to find a church where the pastor would not fall into temptation. I needed a pastor whose heartbeat matched Jesus' in holiness and purity and who was free from judgment.

After crying out to God, I looked up and saw Luis praying and worshiping God wholeheartedly in the dirt. He hadn't finished the pastors' Bible school because he could not read or write, but he was a man full of mercy and compassion. Luis was worshiping with his hands lifted up, adoring the Lord. I held Luis and asked him if he would like to care for these girls as a pastor. He fell apart sobbing, asking if God could give him the privilege and honor of such a beautiful task. Kneeling down, he looked up at me and asked, "Could God have such great love to use a man like me?" He had great humility and great love! He moved to a small new base and began to pastor the girls.

Luis is in heaven now. He died of the AIDS he had contracted in his youth while living on the streets. Luis's life was one of love, mercy and radical forgiveness, poured out in worship for his King. This day, in heaven, he is full of joy with his Bridegroom. "Blessed are the merciful, for they shall receive mercy" (Matthew 5:7).

Jason and Kris, like Luis, have chosen to let go of the ashes of their deep pain and have said a costly yes to God's great exchange. They have chosen to walk in ultimate justice where forgiving and releasing is the standard of righteousness rather than bitterness and revenge. I am so proud of the Vallottons and the way that they have walked in love through an extraordinarily difficult situation. I have watched their lives and have witnessed firsthand how they have chosen to forgive and show extraordinary compassion.

This is ultimate justice: that even in our times of deepest pain, we get the privilege to partner with God in His boundless love and get to experience the height, breadth and depth of His glorious forgiveness flowing through us to others. This is the highest call imaginable and the greatest ministry conceivable, and it is for all of us. It is the call and mandate to love so deeply and so well that it will turn the world upside down!

Heidi Baker, Ph.D.
Founding Director of Iris Ministries
www.irismin.org

Introduction

I never dreamed that any of my children would come to me and break the news my son Jason did the day he visited my office three years ago. And I never imagined that what he had to tell me would trigger one of the worst nightmares in our family's history. Nonetheless, I sat there, stunned, trying my best to absorb his words.

"Dad," he said, "Heather wants a divorce. I think she has someone else!"

For the next 18 months, I watched my son writhe under the intense pain of rejection, abandonment and grief. Day after hard day, I stood by my family as we mostly fumbled about trying to make sense out of the unfathomable. Jason clawed his way forward despite no overt sign of relief. My wife, Kathy, and I did our best to answer the inevitable questions of Jason and Heather's young children—our grandchildren. Kathy and I tried our best to comfort our family, but we were wounded, too—it felt as if we had been harpooned in the very depths of our own souls. I had lost my father when I was three years old and had two stepfathers who abused me, but I had never before experienced pain like this.

Together we cried enough tears for a lifetime.

As we plodded on, something profound began to emerge. It started with Jason, the most wounded of all. As he struggled through the healing process, he received incredible insights. He would say things like, "Dad, God showed me that it's only when we mourn that we are comforted." Jason chose to embrace his pain instead of run from it. At first I questioned the validity of his wholeness. I thought he was living in some sort of denial to help him cope with his extraordinary grief. As time passed, however,

I came to realize that he had taken the most unusual path to wholeness that I had ever seen. Not only was his revelation unusual but it was also working. Jason and my grandchildren were getting well, and joy was filling their lives once again.

It's hard enough to process pain when it is related to a single violation, such as a rape or loss of a loved one, but when a violation continues for years, it tests the true condition of your emotional and spiritual wellbeing. When Heather left, Jason started processing his thoughts through journaling and song writing. Once in a while he would sing me one of his songs or read me something he wrote. His journal was filled with amazing wisdom and deep insights into the process of his wholeness. He began using his new tools as he ministered to people in our ministry school and church family. Before long he was helping hundreds of other people find keys to unlock their own prison doors of pain. When he would share his journey from the podium, people would line up to tell him their own stories and then listen to his wisdom. Now Jason shares his insights and wisdom in this book.

A family psychologist didn't write *The Supernatural Power of Forgiveness*. Instead, it was penned by two people—a son whose heart was broken into a million tiny pieces when the woman of his dreams showed up pregnant with another man's baby, and by his father who loved them both. The insights came to Jason, and he is the one who lived them out, so he writes much of the book. I added two chapters of my own and insights and reflections in some of the others.

Our prayer and sincere desire is that the words of this book would become your path to wholeness and joy. May God Himself meet you as you read and lead you into the palace of your dreams.

Kris Vallotton
Father of a restored family

The *Story* of a *Thousand Lives*

Ever since I (Jason) was a little kid, I have had a passion to bring restoration to the broken. I can still remember the first time I heard the stories about King David's mighty men (see 2 Samuel 23:8-39). I sat there wide-eyed at the kitchen table while my dad told me of their amazing exploits. My heart pounded—not at the thought of slaying a thousand men with only my armor bearer (although that is somewhere in a boy's dream), but at the fact that these men who were known as "mighty" were once the outcasts of their society; they were the nobodies, the violators who weren't welcome in their town!

That day I was overwhelmed with compassion for the lost. The stories of a few broken men made whole gripped my heart, and I made a silent decision to dedicate my life to restoring the brokenhearted, even if they were the ones who were most responsible for the brokenness around them.

Over the past five years as a pastor, I have heard a myriad stories from all types of people. Most of the stories I have heard you would never wish upon your worst enemy. But each story (including mine) contains a golden thread of redemption interwoven in the fabric of their lives. In school, we are taught how to climb the ladder of intellectual success. We are carefully groomed to position ourselves for promotion, adopting the mindset that a person's happiness lies in the ability to create monetary success and financial stability. However, I have found that in spite of countless hours of study and filling our brains with dreams of achievement, we are often left wondering how to do real life.

The way that God designed life was never meant to be rocket science, nor should it have taken a book to understand it all. I believe that we are first spirit beings that have a body. Beyond our flesh and bones is the DNA of God Himself. His Word says it best: "So God created man in his own image . . . male and female he created them" (Genesis 1:27).

WE WERE CREATED FOR INTIMATE
FELLOWSHIP WITH GOD AND WITH EACH
OTHER. BUT SHOMEHOW, WE HAVE LOST WHAT
IT MEANS TO LIVE IN INTIMACY.

We were created for intimate fellowship with God and with each other. But somehow, we have lost what it means to live in intimacy. The average person has no idea where to go or what to do when love has grown cold.

A case in point comes from my own journal. It will make more sense to you when you have read the whole story. But for now, just listen to the heart of it:

12/14/09 1:17 A.M.
So here I lay, comforted by the familiarity of my own bed, a place that has known all of me. I've put Josh Garrels's music on repeat in hopes his lyrics will bring some sense of stability

to the insecurity I am now feeling. Soon, my mind will slow to that of a leisurely lull, and shortly thereafter, I will have wandered my way down that monotonous path in my brain once again. . . . How long will I have to wait for you? When will I find you? If only I had a dollar for every time I have asked these two questions, I could probably start my own foundation to comfort the brokenhearted. The problem with being in this exact spot is that no theoretical answers can quench the desire these questions create. The only thing that will suffice is to actually experience new love again, whenever that happens.

Today as I sit in almost the exact same place as I did the day I wrote that journal entry, I feel the weight of the past two years resting in the back of my head, reminding me of where I've been. Josh Garrels has been placed on repeat again, singing back to me all the memories of the past few years that are carried in this song. Although I can still remember the endless days of pain and my broken heart, the major difference between then and now is that I'm no longer trapped in that place of pain. It is for this very reason that I'm writing today.

My story is the story of a thousand lives. The dream of white picket fences and clean sidewalks that were supposed to be my fortress, protecting me from the evils of a world gone mad. I walked the thin line of safety, struggling to weigh out each decision, knowing that in them lay the ability to affect my future; and yet, as careful as I was, somehow heartache found its way to my front door.

Having firsthand experience with devastating heartbreak, it is my greatest desire to help those who are dealing with the pain of a broken life. By sharing the details of my own story and my path to wholeness, I hope to lead others back to the innocence

in which God created them and encourage them to be powerful people, in every situation, regardless of what they've done or
what has been done to them.

So, no matter what you have done or where you have been,
how high you have climbed or how far you have fallen, there
is a road back to wholeness, and today can be your first step
toward that end.

CHAPTER I

Head Over *Heels*

My story is one of humble beginnings. I (Jason) was raised in the little mountain town of Weaverville, California. (Anyone who comes from a place called "Weaverville" has a fair amount of catching up to do in life!) However, as much as I like to make a bit of fun of that hillbilly place, it was in that town that my heart would learn to love; and it was there that my individuality was formed as I journeyed through adolescence into manhood. Historically, Weaverville was the pot of gold at the end of the rainbow, a place where men tempted fate in pursuit of their dreams. Our town was birthed in the gold-rush era. People from all over came to gamble all they had in hopes of striking it rich. Most of these men started with nothing, and most left with nothing except for the invaluable experience life forged into them, a story much like my own.

Like *Little House on the Prairie*

My family is the kind that any kid might wish for. With three other siblings (two older sisters and an older brother), and two incredible, loving parents, there wasn't a lot left to be desired. I've always likened our family to the one on *Little House on the Prairie*. In all of my growing-up years, I can only remember one time when my parents had a heated argument; and even when they had a disagreement, we all knew my dad would apologize for being wrong and it would all be over.

Drama in our house looked like the time when a bear tried to come through our window because my mom had prayed it would come closer. Who even does that? Or when my neighbor came unglued because my dog walked on his freshly cleaned cement with his muddy paws. In all honesty, my neighbor needed some anger management classes, like the world needs Jesus. Somehow, he forgot that we lived in "Red-Dirt-Ville, California," where it's impossible to keep cement clean, no matter how mad you get.

DRAMA IN OUR HOUSE LOOKED LIKE THE TIME WHEN A BEAR TRIED TO COME THROUGH OUR WINDOW BECAUSE MY MOM HAD PRAYED IT WOULD COME CLOSER. WHO EVEN DOES THAT?

Now, I don't want to paint a picture that there weren't any hard times in our home; it's just that I didn't see most of it. It wasn't until I was much older that I began to realize how much it cost my parents for us to live there.

My parents owned and operated several businesses, all of which were in the automotive industry. Automobile repair has been in my dad's blood since he was young. It was a skill he learned by following his grandpa around on the farm as a little boy. My great-grandpa was a good ol' boy. False teeth, a pair of coveralls and a huge heart are the main words that I would use to describe him. He was the only man who gave my dad any sense of fatherly love as he was growing up, mostly due to the fact that at the young age of three, his own dad drowned while trying to swim his capsized boat back to shore—a loss that left the family impoverished and emotionally scarred. It would be years before that trauma in my dad's life found a resting place. His passion for cars became a beacon of hope in the midst of the storm. It was in this place that he connected with the love of his grandpa and felt most alive.

The automotive business would prove to be a trying one. Although my dad was the best mechanic in town, and arguably the best for miles around, we lived in a town of 3,000 people where the main industry was logging. My parents spent 20-plus years in the industry, operating auto parts stores and service stations, mostly following the rainbow to the pot of gold like so many before them. And, like many others, we left those times with not much more than the wisdom that hard times bring and the hopes of a brighter horizon.

There was always enough at our house, especially enough love; but it was the blood, sweat and tears that produced the harvest. My father could often be found pacing the floor in the early hours of the morning the day before payroll was due, praying and wondering how he was going to make ends meet. It was a huge task for a man who started with nothing.

Will I Ever Fall in Love?

My dad is my hero; he's my best friend and always has been. Like most father-son relationships, we created traditions we followed closely that helped bond us together. One tradition dates as far back as I can remember. Every time I would get into our car with my dad, we would *always* talk about girls. We would cover every subject from how to treat a lady to what qualities I was looking for in a woman. My dad was a master at drawing information out of me without my being fully aware of it. I call it the "Jedi mind trick." Before I even knew what was going on, I'd leaked the information and the damage was done. I was now entering into an embarrassing conversation, one with sweaty palms and a raspy throat. I can remember cringing in my seat a little bit in anticipation of the questions that were about to be directed my way. The funny thing about all of this is that these are my fondest childhood memories. As much as I dreaded that time, I loved it even more.

My story of love really began on one of those car rides with my dad. For years, every Wednesday night, we would take the 20-mile trek through the mountains to Lewiston to go play basketball and love on some juvenile delinquent kids. This provided us with a lot of "in the car" quality time as we made the journey back and forth each week.

On one particular trip, my dad and I were discussing the theory of love between a man and a woman. I was 15 years old and full of questions. We had had this conversation a hundred times before, but this night was different. I started to feel something that I had never felt before. I felt a longing to love and to be loved by a woman. Up until that point, I had a marginal interest in girls, but mostly my drive for hunting had consumed all of the available space in my brain that would normally be used to process the lady kind. Now here I was, beginning to wonder out loud as I discovered this pulling in my heart: "Dad, am I ever going to fall in love?" I know what you're thinking; you're saying to yourself, *He's only 15. What's the big hurry?*

It helps if you understand that in our family, men fall in love young. My dad set the trend when he asked my mom to marry him when she was just 13 years old. Being the opportunist that he is, my father felt there was no need to waste time in fumbling with all of the pointless details that dating can incur. He was set on her, so he sealed the deal then and there!

So there I sat, spilling out my heart, desperately trying to find some hope to cure this longing in me. "Will I ever fall in love?" My father answered me that night with full confidence, "Yes, you will, son. You will fall in love."

Somehow, my dad's answer revealed a deeper question in my soul: *Do I have what it takes to fall in love?* As I pondered the matter, my heart wrenched with uncertainty.

A Princess in a Secondhand Life

It's funny how often the seasons of my life have changed without my having any awareness until change smacks me square in the face. When that happens, I feel like a ship that's been hit by a rogue wave, and I'm left scrambling to find my bearings in the midst of the chaos. This particular change of season would prove to be no different.

She was a beauty queen, something that I had never seen before. Well, at least not looking back at me. She had all the makings of someone who could draw out the moron in me. You know what I'm talking about—just her looking in my general direction left me fumbling for words, like the guy who stumbles over every hurdle in the hundred-yard dash, a pitiful sight for all who witness it. For some reason, I could not get my brain to connect with the rest of my body while standing in her presence. I kept reminding myself about the story of the Tortoise and the Hare, "Slow and steady wins the race." After all, she was living at my best friend's house.

The story of how I met Heather is quite interesting, and maybe a little bit confusing too. My best friend in high school (and still to this day) is Jerome Evans. Jerome's parents (Wes and Kathy) have big hearts for people who could use a hand up in life. They were notorious for taking in all kinds of kids who needed a place to stay and who were longing for some good old-fashioned love. One of those kids ended up being Amanda McKay, Heather's best friend. Amanda, like Heather, was also one of those girls who could draw the stupid out of you. With long blonde hair and big blue eyes, she was "the girl" on the cheerleading team that gave guys a reason to stay at the basketball game long after we were getting our butts handed to us.

One of the most beautiful attributes about Amanda was not just that she could light up the room, but how she loved God. She was an inspiration to all who were around her, especially to Heather, and also to the guys who wanted to date her. But let me get back to Heather.

A Child in a Grown-up's World

Heather grew up in a broken home. Harsh words and absent love were the norm for her. In those years, her mom was emotionally checked out, unable to care for the needs of a child, and her dad was somewhere beyond the Canadian border, chasing a new dream. Most of her youth was spent living from house to house, usually ending up at her grandma's or her aunt's place. As time went on, she began to grow weary of this nomad life. She needed a new beginning, a place where she could find the peace that stability brings. So, at 16, with high hopes and the promise of a new horizon, she packed her bags and headed east to Salt Lake City, a child in a grown-up's world.

It wasn't long before her schedule was in full swing. A 60-hour-a-week job and early mornings consumed most of her available time. Soon, the grueling hours and a lack of friends began to take its toll. The grass was not as green as she had thought it would be.

Once again, Heather had reached an all-time low, and once again she was ready for a change. It was about that time that Amanda went to visit her in Utah. Amanda, being her upbeat, contagious self, always brought Heather so much hope. The love of her best friend was something Heather needed so deeply in this season.

AMANDA, BEING HER UPBEAT, CONTAGIOUS SELF, ALWAYS BROUGHT HEATHER SO MUCH HOPE. THE LOVE OF HER BEST FRIEND WAS SOMETHING HEATHER NEEDED SO DEEPLY IN THIS SEASON.

Over the next few weeks, Heather began to realize how much she was missing out. She started thinking about how Amanda had two great parents who loved her, something Heather so desperately lacked. The decision at hand was not rocket science; Heather knew that she needed what Amanda had. I'm sure that Wes and Kathy were probably expecting it, and even if they weren't, they welcomed the phone call from Amanda. "Dad, can you come pick up Heather and me? She wants to live with us."

On the way home from Utah, Heather experienced the joy that Amanda had in her life by giving her heart to the Lord. Up to now she had been "wandering" through this world, a princess in a secondhand life. This was the new beginning she had been frantically looking for.

Head Over Heels

The news of her arrival got my full attention. I had met Heather when I was about 14. I can remember that moment even to this day. She was sitting in the park grass on a blanket that she had knitted by hand. With her flowing brown hair and deep green eyes, and wearing a rockin' red-and-brown sweater, she was looking *ah-may-zing*. It was the Fourth of July, and I was the luckiest guy around, because I was with the blonde-haired, blue-eyed Amanda *and* her best friend. *Thank You, Jesus!* Needless to say, I was a little bit excited to hear about Heather not only moving back to town and becoming born again, but also moving into my best friend's house. There was only one problem: At this time in my life, I was not what you would call the "jock." I was pretty much a nerd!

After I had that "conversation" in the car with my dad about finding love, I had been spending a fair amount of time in pursuit of a lady friend. However, in a town of 3,000, your options of finding "the one" are considerably limited, especially when you're the guy who's still praying for puberty to kick in. Here I was, 16 years old, and desperately trying to induce the maturing process as quickly as possible. My thought was that squeaking my voice on every other word would help to jump-start testosterone in me. I'm not sure if it was really all that effective, but desperate times call for desperate measures, and right then times were getting desperate. I had heard that Heather was back in town, and I needed to do something fast!

Our relationship started off as pretty much nonexistent, unless you include the fact that I spent every night at their house (with my best friend, Jerome). I knew deep down inside there was no way in God's green earth that Heather was going to fall for a guy like me. As a matter of fact, my friends felt the same way, including Heather's best friend, Amanda.

I can remember having a conversation with Amanda's boyfriend, who was also my best pal on the basketball team. I was expressing to him that I was a little bit interested in Heather. Actually I think I said that she was killing me. He basically laughed and said, "You're dreaming; she would never go for you." Heather was used to having guys chase her who could throw a football 400 yards and run the 40 in less than a second. You know what I'm talking about . . . the guys you're not even allowed to look at because your eyeballs will melt out of your head . . . those guys. And here I was, working on my squeaking voice. Looking back, I can see that my friends weren't being mean; they were just trying to protect me from the inevitable.

I'm not the kind of guy who gives up at the first sign of opposition. When push comes to shove, I know how to put on a little Old Spice and take a shower every other day. It's all about staying the course, making sure I'm bringing my A game to the home field with every opportunity I get.

Heather and I usually saw each other about five or six days a week because we were in youth group and church together (not to mention that I practically lived at Jerome's house). The more time I spent with her, the more I was beginning to fall head over heels for this girl. After all, she was amazingly beautiful, really funny, loved sports and going for long walks on the beach, and she smelled so good (that's not always a given in Weaverville). However, the thing that attracted me to her the most was the relationship she had with the Lord. This girl was glowing! She had come out of such a deep place of brokenness and loneliness into a place of freedom in just a short period of time. I have never seen someone make a transition like that before in my life, even now. She had only been saved for two months and she was absolutely on fire. Every day I watched this girl transform before my eyes.

In Love

Two months had passed since Heather had moved into the Evans's house, and I was not sure how much more of this torture I could take. This girl was workin' me every day! Just about the time I decided to put my heart away for safe keeping, I got the news that I had waited my whole life to hear. It all happened one night at our local coffee shop (The Mamma Llama). This was the place where all the "cool kids" in the youth group hung out on Saturday nights. Most of the other kids in school were at parties, drinking it up and playing tonsil hockey, but not us youth group kids. We were at the coffee shop sipping on Italian sodas.

So there I was just hanging out with all of my friends. The night was running late, and I was badly in need of a change of scenery. After a few suggestions, Jerome and I and a few other people decided to head over to my house for a bit. While we were in the car, Jerome proceeded to tell me that he had the best news I've ever heard in my life! Now, I already knew what he was going to say. He was going to tell me that he had a new Remington 11-87 shotgun on order for duck season, and if I'm lucky, he was going to let me have a go with it.

To my surprise, he proceeded to tell me that he had cornered Heather in the coffee shop and asked her what she thought about me. The next 10 minutes of this story are a blur, kind of like watching *The Matrix* when Neo was dodging those bullets. While I was driving, Jerome belted out, "She thinks you're cute!"

I AM CUTE!! (*car swerving everywhere*). I'm not sure that I had ever had this feeling before, but right at that moment, I went into full *Matrix* mode; the world slowed to a snail's pace and it was like I could count every letter that came out of his mouth. I was completely engulfed in the serenity of that moment. *Someone likes me— the someone whom I have wanted more than any other someone.*

There's only one thing that a guy can do in this situation. I had to go back to Mamma Llama and drive Heather home! Without any hesitation, I turned the car around and dropped all of my friends off at the nearest location (which is any location in Weaverville). After a few "good luck" wishes, I mustered up my courage. After all, she is the girl that brings the "moron" out in me. I knew full well what was about to happen to me the second I stepped a foot in there. I knew that she was going to look in my general direction, and in that instant, my knees would be eligible to play with the half-time marching band at the Rose Bowl.

I WAS COMPLETELY ENGULFED IN THE SERENITY OF THAT MOMENT. SOMEONE LIKES ME—THE SOMEONE WHOM I HAVE WANTED MORE THAN ANY OTHER SOMEONE.

With sweaty palms, my knees playing the "Military March" and my heart beating at 10,000 RPM a second, I carefully made my way to her. I kept telling myself, *Slow and steady wins the race; don't try to eat a whole cow in one bite; just say something small like "Hey, how are you?"*

By the time the night had worn down, we had held a whole conversation full of one-liners and good laughs. The only thing left to do here was to drive her home. My Pontiac 6000 is about the only thing I had up on this girl. That car was not the flashiest piece of machinery in the world, but it had been with me through thick and thin. Actually, just a few weeks before that night, I used it to transport a deer I had killed while hunting. This car had been the faithful participant of many first dates in our family, mostly because it was a hand-me-down from my parents to all of my siblings; and because I'm the youngest in my family, it's safe to say that this car had seen better days. However, Heather didn't have a car, so for me, this was the perfect opportunity to capitalize on the situation. "Would you like a ride home?" I squeaked out nervously. With a quick acceptance from her, we were off to her house.

On the way home, I knew that I had about two minutes to work up enough courage to ask her out. In Weaverville, everything is within a five-minute drive, so I had to work fast. I'm pretty sure that I have the same determination my dad does when it comes to sealing the deal. Once I know that I want something, I have to have it without delay.

ON THE WAY HOME, I KNEW THAT I HAD ABOUT
TWO MINUTES TO WORK UP ENOUGH COURAGE
TO ASK HER OUT. IN WEAVERVILLE,
EVERYTHING IS WITHIN A FIVE-MINUTE DRIVE,
SO I HAD TO WORK FAST.

Later, my microwave mentality would come back to haunt me, but not on this night. By the time we pulled into her driveway, I had worked myself up to the fact that if I didn't ask this girl to go out with me, the sun was going to fall out of the sky and the whole earth was going to catch on fire. So I popped the question: "Um . . . uh, I would really like you . . . I mean, I would really like to take you out sometime, if that's okay with you?"

She responded more confidently than I did. "Yeah, I would love it!"

"Okay. How about Saturday at six?"

"Yeah, that would be great!"

I'm so glad that there wasn't a camera in the car that night on the drive home from her house. That would have made the YouTube million-plus view count for sure. It was all I could do to keep myself from driving a hundred miles an hour in circles.

Instead, I just screamed at the top of my lungs and pounded on my steering wheel in exhilaration. I had just asked out the woman of my dreams, and she said YES!

The Road to Destiny Lane

It wasn't long into our relationship that we discovered our love for each other. As a matter of fact, I think it was on the seventh day of our "relationship" that we exchanged the "I love yous!" She was in love with me, and I was in love with her. This was a match made in heaven! Over the next two years, Heather and I began to build a relationship to last a lifetime. Both of us were determined to sow strength and love into each other. We were dedicated to the success of our relationship and our future together.

Heather and I started off strong; we had our purity plan on lockdown, and we were now well on our way to the marriage suite. Everything was amazing until about six months before our wedding date. Heather and I had grown up worlds apart. I was one of the kids from *Little House on the Prairie*, and she was the little girl left to fend for herself. All through high school, I was the guy who wore white T-shirts every day because I wanted to remind myself that I was pure. At 13 years old, I made a covenant with God that I was going to keep myself sexually pure until the day I was married. Heather didn't have the same opportunity or the upbringing that would allow for that type of lifestyle.

Looking back, everything is crystal clear. There came a point inside of Heather when she decided she couldn't go through with the wedding. Totally broken, she called my dad one afternoon, asking if she could meet with him. My dad, who loves Heather just like one of his own kids, dropped what he was doing and invited her over. When she arrived, he could tell that she had been crying for quite some time. Through her tears, she began to explain how she couldn't be with someone who had never done anything wrong when she had lived such a torn-up life. It just didn't feel right.

My dad, full of compassion, began to explain to her how Jesus' death on the cross heals our heart and forgives our sins. He explained that when we ask God for forgiveness, our sins aren't even remembered anymore; they are totally wiped clean.

That day was a turning point in Heather's life; she felt clean for the first time in years. Because of the cross, she finally had something worth fighting for—her purity! Just six months later, we exchanged our wedding vows. That was the most beautiful day of my life. There she was, riding in on a strong brown horse, fully captivating everyone in her cream-colored wedding dress, and she was all mine. Life for us had just begun.

Life in the Fast Lane

At 18, what does a person really know about life? Every 18-year-old thinks he has it all figured out; but for me it didn't take long to find out that life was about to happen to me, like it or not. This would be the story of our marriage for the next nine years.

Heather and I enjoyed a short honeymoon, and now life was in full swing. We lived in a quaint little white two-bedroom house in Weaverville. I was working for my dad, delivering auto parts, and Heather was taking care of the books for my mom. I'm not sure if you've ever worked for family before, but it can be the best and the worst experience ever. As glad as I was to see my parents every day, I hated the monotony of delivering auto parts. What kind of future is there in that? However, if there is anything my dad has taught me about life, it's to start at the bottom and work your way up to the top. That's something he's a master at, and that would be something I would hold fast to for the rest of my life.

Like the pace of everything else in our life, we started having kids right off the bat. Just two months after we were married, we were pregnant. What an answer to prayer: we were going to have a child! On August 23, 1999, I became a father to Elijah Cannon Vallotton. This was truly the best day of our lives.

IF THERE IS ANYTHING MY DAD HAS TAUGHT ME ABOUT LIFE, IT'S TO START AT THE BOTTOM AND WORK YOUR WAY UP TO THE TOP. THAT WOULD BE SOMETHING I WOULD HOLD FAST TO FOR THE REST OF MY LIFE.

By the time I was 24, the manger was full of kids, and life was moving at breakneck speeds. Heather was a stay-at-home mom with our three kids while I brought home the bread.

From Boyhood to Manhood

Looking back, it's amazing how fast the seasons in my life changed as I went from being newly married and delivering auto parts, to being a dad of three and ready to begin my dream vocation. We moved to Redding, California, and within five years I was working my dream job. For as long as I can remember, I have wanted to pastor people. I never wanted to be the head honcho who preaches every week, but rather a vital member of a larger team. Ever since I was a little boy, I have had such a heart to transform broken people into their God-given identity.

In 2005, I made that transition and became a pastor at Bethel Church's Bible college. Life for Heather and me had never been better. We had made it all the way from courtship to marriage and through the tests that time brings. With three beautiful kids, a dream job and a new horizon, we were home!

Chapter 2

Hell Has Come to *Breakfast*

There are so many moments that we live on this earth only to forget them the very next day. This isn't one of those moments. Although I can't tell you the date and time, I can clearly remember what happened. I had begun reading a book called *1776*—historian David McCullough's fascinating perspective on the beginning of the Revolutionary War. I wouldn't call myself a book buff, or anything even close to that. Actually, if a book is more than 300 pages, that's usually enough to deter me from reading it. However, after briefly picking up the book, I couldn't put it down. My heart was captured by the stories of our fearless forefathers who gave everything they had to gain our freedom as a nation. These men had something worth living for.

Looking back on that time of reading about America's struggle, I was absolutely clueless as to what my heart was being prepared for; I had no idea that in just a few months, my whole life was going to fall apart, and I would get the opportunity of a lifetime to deal with the kind of pain that builds character.

A Prayer for Change

So there I was on that fateful day, driving down Benton street, just thinking to myself, *I want the character of George Washington . . .*

Now if I were smart, I would have stopped my thoughts right there. But for some reason, I did what no one should ever do if he or she hasn't counted the cost: I moved that idea from my brain to my lips. Before I could stop myself, I said to the Lord out loud, "I want the character of George Washington."

I'm not sure exactly why it always happens this way, but it does. You can pray a thousand prayers, but it seems like the one the Lord decides to answer is the one you should *never* have prayed (probably something to do with building character).

YOU CAN PRAY A THOUSAND PRAYERS, BUT IT SEEMS LIKE THE ONE THE LORD DECIDES TO ANSWER IS THE ONE YOU SHOULD NEVER HAVE PRAYED.

If I had thought about it a little bit longer, I would have realized for what I was asking. George Washington was not a man who lived an untested life. He wrote a letter to his mom in 1755, after the French and Indian War, saying that he had escaped uninjured, but "I had four bullet holes in my coat and two horses shot out from under me." It's said of George that he believed he couldn't die until his "appointed time," so he would do these crazy feats of valor against all odds, with little to no fear. And here I was, praying that I would have character like him.

Well, as the Bible says, "Ask and it will be given to you" (Luke 11:9). I was asking, and I did receive! I'm not sure if you have ever shared a similar experience, but in about four months' time, my life was completely set on fire. Everything that had been stable soon began to shake. This process began when a very close family member went through a horrific nervous breakdown. I spent countless hours in prayer and phone conversation with this person contending for breakthrough, believing that peace was just around the corner.

I had done a lot of counseling in my job, and I had helped people through these types of issues before. But two months later, another family member suffered a similar attack. *What was going on?*

This whole process started in October 2007, and now it was December. Sometimes I'm not the most spiritually "in tune" person, but even I could tell that *hell had come to breakfast.* My hopes were that this visit was just one meal. Unfortunately, it was only the beginning of what would take almost two years to walk through.

When the Temperature Dropped

So there I was, literally in the middle of winter, but I was also slowly beginning to feel colder inside than I had ever felt before. I had never had one close family member go through something like this, let alone two at the same time. As the days passed, I realized there wasn't going to be a quick fix. Their dark night of the soul had seemingly come to stay.

There is no feeling quite like that of being a powerless bystander to a total disaster. Watching your loved ones, day in and day out, tremble under the thought of having to face another morning does something to a man's soul. Momentum is a force to be reckoned with. Once the train gets going, it's a bear to stop, and things were about to get worse!

February rolled around, and it had been four months since the beginning of all of this. I welcomed the new month with open arms. I was hoping for crisp morning air and freedom from those long, dark nights that had been such a constant weight.

As the month began to unfold, it was not long before I started to realize that I was feeling more alone at home than usual. One thing you need to understand is that feeling alone in my house is almost an impossibility. I have three kids: Evan, my youngest, was four; Rilie, my princess, was six; and Elijah, my oldest, was eight; and of course my beautiful wife, Heather, to whom I had been married for nine years. Alone time at my house existed only between the hours of 12:00 A.M. and 6:00 A.M., if I was lucky. The other 18 hours were spent filling sippy cups, playing WWE (World Wrestling Entertainment) in the living room and tending to every need that has ever been known to man. There is never a dull moment around here! However, my "alone at home" feeling was not produced from the absence of people, but rather from the absence of connection.

AT FIRST, I WAS NOT ALL THAT CONCERNED ABOUT MY EMOTIONAL STATE OF BEING. THIS WAS NOT THE FIRST TIME I HAD FELT LONELY IN MY HOUSE, AND I WAS SURE IT WAS NOT GOING TO BE THE LAST.

If you have been married for any significant amount of time, you know this is not a freak incident, but rather a season you sometimes go through as lovers. At first, I was not all that concerned about my emotional state of being. This was not the first time I had felt lonely in my house, and I was sure it was not going to be the last.

There were so many contributing factors that were feeding into the feelings I had going on inside. Some of it was due to my wife's car accident. She was cut off while driving 70 MPH down the freeway and was broadsided by an SUV, leaving her with four broken ribs, a punctured lung and some broken teeth. Although she had recovered from that a while ago, her ribs would act up sometimes, causing her to sleep on the couch for a few weeks at a time. As you could probably guess, that wasn't helping our connection at all.

On my end of the deal, I felt a lot of pressure due to what my family was going through, and it was threatening my overall sense of peace. Plus, I was the father of three very energetic kids. So there we were, going through one of those times when you need the commitment part of love to kick in and pull you close.

After about a week of feeling lonely, I realized this wasn't going to go away on its own. I needed to let Heather know where I was so she could help remedy our lack of connection. Heather was always pretty good about listening to where I was at and working on her end of the deal to connect with me. We never really had a problem with being able to share feelings and somehow work it out. However, this time was painfully different. The more I began to open up and let her know where I was at, the further away she seemed. I felt like we were magnets that had somehow gotten flipped around, and connecting had become an impossible feat. At this point, I knew I was in over my head and in need of intervention.

Something Is Seriously Wrong

During the past year-and-a-half, Heather and I had been going to counseling once a month. Unlike most people, I don't believe in waiting to get help when all four tires are flat and the engine is on fire; and I strongly believe in learning and growing from other people's successes. One of my spiritual fathers is our on-staff family counselor at Bethel Church, and because we are family to him, we had access to meet with him on a regular basis. Being the smart man that I am, or mostly just being a week into feeling totally overwhelmed and disconnected, I sent out the SOS call to Danny.

Danny's office was a place that I had grown accustomed to, and I was thinking that this meeting was going to be like the previous ones. Heather and I had never really had too much trouble in our marriage; well, we didn't fight or anything like that. So I figured that I would share my side of the story and she would share hers; then Danny would do his magic and we would be good to go. At least that's what I was hoping for.

As soon as we sat down, Danny asked Heather to share what had been going on in her heart. The first words out of her mouth were, "Jason, do you want to leave the room, or do you want to stay for this?" She had not opened up to me at all that past week, and I suddenly realized she was getting ready to uncork a bottle of pain. Totally scared of what was to come, I cautiously asked her to continue. Through a mouth full of tears, she began to say, "I have never been in love with you, I don't have any vision for our future and I don't feel like you have any passion. I feel like I'm slowly dying in this relationship."

As she continued to speak, I just looked at her, wondering what she was even talking about. How does a person come to a conclusion after nine years of marriage and three kids that there has never been a spark in the relationship? How can she think that I have no passion for her or for my life? I have served this woman every day, from the moment we met, with love and respect. I left that meeting more hurt and confused than I have ever been in my entire life. The only woman whom I have ever loved had just told me that she had *never* loved me. I learned that heavy is the heart that loves, and painful are the demands of intimacy.

A Change of Heart

I left Danny's office that day with instructions to win her heart;
I needed to recreate the youthful spark we once had. Danny
likened our situation to driving an outdated automobile. He
explained that if a couple drives an old Volkswagen beetle for
their entire life and then one day takes a Porsche for a ride, they
could easily say that before driving a Porsche, they had never
driven a car before. Maybe it wasn't that Heather didn't love
me; maybe it was that our relationship had been an old beat-up
car driving down a lonely road, and now we needed some refur-
bishing. If there was ever a time in my life when I needed to
muster up some courage, this was the time. I had to bring my
A game, and quick! I needed to work up some type of flawless
plan to get this woman to connect with me again, if not for my
sake, then for the sake of our kids.

> IF THERE WAS EVER A TIME IN MY LIFE
> WHEN I NEEDED TO MUSTER UP SOME
> COURAGE, THIS WAS THE TIME. I HAD TO
> BRING MY A GAME, AND QUICK!

I started by first working on our connection. With my heart
in my hands, I began to pursue her. Over the course of the next
two months, I spent loads of time thinking and praying about
and acting on plans that I had carefully formulated to break
into her heart. I made attempt after attempt to find the combi-
nation—everything from dinner dates to paying special attention to speak to her in her love languages (the things I can do
that make her feel the most cherished), but the safe that was
her heart could not be cracked. She was locked up tight and the

key was nowhere to be found. *If only I could figure it out.* Heather was slowly moving out of my life; she had all but packed her bags and left.

As I've reread my journal entries of that time, I realize how painfully distant and confusing our lives had become.

Journal Entry: 4/16/08

I just finished talking with Heather tonight. She is still feeling like she wants to be somewhere else when I am around. She says that we just see most everything in a different way. I asked her what it was that was so different, but she would not tell me. She said it is not like we can just change it and then we are all better and connected. I said I understand that and I am not trying to change so that we are all better, but I am trying to understand what she sees as different. I told her tonight that she is a good woman, and she said, "You don't have to say that." I think she really has a hard time right now feeling like she has put me through hell, and now she is doing it again with not feeling like she is in love with me, so that makes her feel not so good. She is an amazing woman, and even through this I love her and see the good in her. She is strong and full of life. She said that she wants to feel alive. I asked her why she wasn't feeling alive, and she could not answer me. I know that feeling alive is an inside job; that it's nothing that I can fix for her. She needs to find it for herself if she's going to find it at all. She has more freedom than she has ever had, and if she is feeling like she is not alive and is just surviving, that is pretty crappy for her. I don't want you to live like that, Heather; I want you to live a full, loving life.

As time passed, it was looking like my love for Heather was not going to be enough. For so long, our simple connection was all that we needed; but now my best effort was far from satisfying to her. What had happened that would cause her to not even want to work on us? This whole thing was not adding up.

My Dark Reality

On April 22, Heather went to stay at her grandma's cabin for the weekend so she could get alone for a bit and process. After a couple of days away, she returned in the same condition she had left . . . distant. I had finally come to the place where I started to believe that it wasn't me, and there wasn't something that I could do to fix this mess. If I had cheated on her or been abusive, I would have understood the disconnection and her unwillingness to work on us. But to have her pull so far away on purpose when she had a great husband and kids made no sense to me.

> I HAD FINALLY COME TO THE PLACE
> WHERE I STARTED TO BELIEVE THAT IT WASN'T
> ME, AND THERE WASN'T SOMETHING THAT
> I COULD DO TO FIX THIS MESS.

When she returned from her weekend away, I told her I was having a hard time trusting her and I was going to look in her stuff to try to figure out what was going on. I'm not the type of person to snoop around, and I didn't want to go behind her back, but I couldn't stay in this place any longer.

A few weeks earlier, she had changed all of her passwords on the computer, which felt really weird to me since it was just her and me using it. Also, we had had some issues in the past with her not being fully open with me on some major things. I was beginning to feel totally unsafe, and I needed to figure out why.

The more I began to search for answers, the darker my reality became. I was finding things that were terminal to the health of our relationship, things that induced shaking throughout my entire body. The details have been left out for the sake of our kids, but the outcome remains the same. All of my searching led me to discover that she had been having an ongoing affair with one of my friends from high school. The first few paragraphs of my journal entry from that day quickly remind me of the pain my discovery inflicted.

Journal Entry: 5/1/08

You ask me if I am okay, if I need to talk. I woke up to this nightmare: My wife loves another man; she has given herself fully to him. Oh, how I wish this were all a bad dream! What was supposed to be mine has become his. Have you ever been betrayed? Have you ever been cut to the bone, stabbed in the back? Have you ever given someone your whole heart only to find out they used your heart to beat you with it? Have you ever laid down your life for someone? Have you ever served with reckless abandonment and in return got back a list of things that you failed to do?

I handed you my life; I put something in your hand that was so special, a gift that you have never had or dreamed of; I gave you my purity, my pure love. I won the battles of my youth; I fought for years to bring you something so pure and true, so genuine, that I don't think you knew what to do with it. Have you ever had a man fight for you? Have you ever felt the security of being fully known by someone who will value what is found? You only show broken people who you really are, only the ones who are expected to accept you because they are in the same boat or worse off. I was never let into that little space, never given the opportunity to break your heart. I was only able to observe from a distance and reminiscence about what it might be like to hold something so guarded that only the broken get to touch it.

Pain as violent as death shot through me. My whole body trembled from head to toe at the realization of what was happening. I stayed up all night begging her to stay with me, completely drunk with fear, wishing I could somehow wake up from this horrible reality. My wife was leaving me for another man; she was leaving our kids and she was leaving my family.

I was fully aware of what was about to happen next. For months, my previous counseling sessions, where I was the counselor and someone else was the counselee who thought his life was over, began rolling through my mind—mostly the ones where the kid tells me how screwed up he is because his parents got a divorce. I knew that soon I was going to sit my kids down and look them in the eyes, and somehow let them know that Mom was not coming home, that Mom chose to leave. I was going to have months of lying in bed with my kids, listening to them cry, while they tried to sort out why their mom didn't want to stay. And I knew that I was going to somehow break the news to the church where I was a pastor that my marriage was ending. I had never felt a more surreal moment in my life than the day she left. Everything we had worked toward in our relationship had just walked out the door with her.

Hell Has Come to Breakfast

All throughout that time when I was reading *1776*, I used to think to myself how lucky a person like George Washington was, not because he didn't die in battle or because he made the history books, but because he had a battle to fight. He had an opportunity to test his mettle and himself with enough courage that death no longer held its sting.

They say that heroes are found on the battlefield, and if what they say is true, I now had my opportunity. There I was, preparing myself to forge the character of George Washington. I had found my battlefield, and two months later I was alone, without my wife, with my whole life completely on fire.

THERE I WAS, PREPARING MYSELF TO FORGE THE CHARACTER OF GEORGE WASHINGTON. I HAD FOUND MY BATTLEFIELD, AND TWO MONTHS LATER I WAS ALONE, WITHOUT MY WIFE, WITH MY WHOLE LIFE ON FIRE.

The fog that surrounded my family members had continued to creep in, and now their depression had reached an all-time low. Hell had come to breakfast, and I was the one who had to decide what to do with it. Much like George Washington, I was in a battle; but I was fighting for the freedom of my family and for the restoration of the life we had once known. Change had come and forced its way through my life, leaving me searching, wondering once again if I had what it takes to withstand the betrayal of a loved one. That was the last time Heather and I would share a home together.

If you are anything like me, you're probably feeling a sense of injustice or anger toward Heather's decisions. Keep reading. In these next few chapters, I will show you how I processed the pain of betrayal and found the true justice that leads to wholeness. It's a pattern that can help you grow through pain and develop strength of character. It's a prayer that God is pleased to answer.

CHAPTER 3

He Who *Holds the Key*

My wife is my shepherd . . . I am in want. She has taken my power because I have given it to her. I am guided in the path of least resistance because there is no comfort for my soul. Even though I walk through the valley of the shadow of death, I fear all the time because she is my source. I must prepare a table for her and have no needs because my happiness depends on hers. Her words and touch comfort me, but only for a minute, because the touch of God is what I really need. Surely powerlessness will follow me all the days of my life because I believe there is only one powerful person in this relationship, and it's not me.

Unfortunately, my story is a far cry from the psalmist's original masterpiece that speaks of God's comfort and loving care. I didn't begin our marriage as a powerless person; the process of giving my power away happened ever so slowly over the course of our relationship. However, I do remember the climax of the story—the day when I realized I needed to do whatever it took to keep Heather in our relationship.

Answering to the Wrong Master

The year was 2004, and I'm positive that it was fall because I can still recall the bright yellow leaves that had collected on the grass. That night, Heather and I had spent the evening enjoying dinner at our friends Amanda and Luke's house. After dinner, the ladies went for a drive while the husbands were left at home to roughhouse with the kids—I mean, take care of the kids. If you're a parent, especially a mom, you know how great those long drives with a girlfriend can be. I assumed that the enjoyment of their peaceful drive was the cause for their delayed return, because it seemed like they were taking forever.

When they finally came back, I noticed that Heather was really somber—something was obviously bugging her. Our drive home was quiet and long; it was one of those times when you know there is more being said in the absence of words than you want to know. Eventually, we arrived home and put the kids to sleep. As we lay in bed that night, Heather told me that she needed to talk to me about something. I had heard that tone of voice before; it always meant, "Brace yourself for what's to come!"

As she unpacked her feelings and all that she had been going through, I felt overwhelmed. She was coming out of a hard season in her life, but I was unable to see that just as a caterpillar turns into a butterfly, she was on the brink of a breakthrough. Unfortunately, I was too unsure of myself to handle where she was at in her life. I lay there for a long time just trying to find the right words to say. I felt powerless, yet I really wanted to jump in and make sure that she was going to be okay. At least that's what I thought at the time. Looking back, I can now see that what I really wanted was to make sure I was going to be all right. I began to buy into a lie that the only way I was going to be fine was to make sure that she was okay.

The details of her challenge don't really matter. The fact is that at some point in life, every married couple goes through challenges that have the opportunity to leave one or both of them feeling powerless. It can stem from a poor decision they made, problems with their children, a tough financial situation, or countless other scenarios. Before you know it, instead of listening to God for direction and strength, you're looking to your spouse to bring security to your soul. Insecurity is actually security rooted in the wrong resource! For me, being a young father with three small kids was enough to make me feel as if my sanity was fragile. It didn't take much for me to let go of God and cling to my wife for stability.

There are a lot of times in life when you think you have "arrived" only to find out you really know nothing at all. I had known the effects of pressure before. I had supervised a firefighting team for a couple of years and was nearly killed twice. I knew the weight of taking care of my men in the midst of danger. I also knew what it feels like to have to provide for a family. But even in all of that, I was still ignorant of this kind of pressure. The thought of my wife wanting to leave me literally made me dizzy. I felt like I was going to pass out from the stress. I had to do something; there is no way that I could live like this.

I finally made a decision to do whatever was necessary to take the pressure off of Heather. I thought that if she had less pressure, then she wouldn't feel as trapped; and if she felt less trapped, she would get better; and if she got better, I would be okay. I needed Heather to be all right so that I would be all right. Thus, I began the process of giving Heather the keys to my happiness.

"MY WIFE IS MY SHEPHERD" BECAME MY MOTTO
FOR THE NEXT FOUR YEARS OF MARRIAGE. FROM
THE OUTSIDE (AND EVEN TO ME), IT ALL FELT SO
REAL AND HUMBLE—SO CHRISTLIKE.

"My wife is my shepherd" became my motto for the next four years of marriage. From the outside (and even to me), it all felt so real and humble—so Christlike. I felt like the amazing husband who could live having little to no needs while being able to serve unconditionally without requiring her to participate in any way she deemed unnecessary. I thought I was being "Jesus" to her by allowing her the time she needed to heal and recover. The only problem was that she had become my source of life.

I should probably stop here and say that Heather did face the wind. A few days after telling me about her struggle, we met with Danny Silk and my parents to seek help. Over the course of a year, she courageously overcame her battle with bulimia. However, even in the midst of her freedom, I still believed a lie that held me bound. Here's what I thought: *If I have needs in this relationship, she will not be able to handle them, and I will be left alone with three kids and a broken heart. I am the one who is responsible to keep her in this relationship, and I am the one who needs to take all of the pressure off of her in order for her to be okay. I am the source of her peace and stability.*

Initially, I saw how giving more and taking some pressure off of Heather was helpful for her recovery, and it was the right thing to do. However, the problem wasn't in my actions to serve her more or require less of her. The problem was that my belief system had become skewed. I had built a partnership with fear, and it had quickly overtaken me.

Whatever you fear will ultimately become your master. This is the process of allowing deception to take control of your mind. It all starts by allowing small, cunning lies to creep in undetected. At first, they seem rational—a vital contribution to the wellbeing of your personhood. They come cloaked in common sense and take up residence inside of logic and reason. But their deception is deep and destructive. Their words have nothing to do with the Father's heart, for they are only a façade of true light.

Entire identities and worldviews can be founded upon lies. Obviously, this is catastrophic to the health and wellbeing of the individual, and it must be undone immediately. To overpower these destructive lies, we must first recognize them as lies. Yet, because we are often oblivious to what is going on inside of us, it can be hard to recognize what is actually driving us.

Who Is in Your "God Spot"?

Psalm 23 paints an amazing picture of what it looks like to have God as the main source of our life, leading us out of the shadow of death.

> The LORD is my shepherd, I shall not be in want. He makes me lie down in green pastures, he leads me beside quiet waters, he restores my soul. He guides me in paths of righteousness for his name's sake. Even though I walk through the valley of the shadow of death, I will fear no evil, for you are with me; your rod and your staff, they comfort me. You prepare a table before me in the presence of my enemies. You anoint my head with oil; my cup overflows. Surely goodness and love will follow me all the days of my life, and I will dwell in the house of the LORD forever (Ps. 23:1-6).

These few verses are a powerful revelation of what happens to us when God is our master and main source of strength. Not only are we led to a place of quiet rest, but we are also restored in that place. The beautiful part of this passage is that it covers all of life, and even death. David says, "Even though I walk through the valley of the shadow of death, I will fear no evil, for you are with me; your rod and your staff, they comfort me." I want you to notice that he did not say that God is his Shepherd because He bails him out of bad situations; rather, God is the director and the source of his life in every circumstance.

God is the Shepherd of our lives, even when we walk through the valley of the shadow of death. Therefore, the peace of God wraps around us while He leads the way. One of the best ways we can find out who is leading us is to stop and take a look at our everyday life. What has become our main source of direction, protection, comfort, healing and identity? Where do we go on a daily basis to get our needs met? Ask yourself those questions. Your answers will reveal a lot about *what* or *who* is in your "God" spot.

The danger here is that it's so easy to think that God is in control of our lives when it's sunny out and the daisies are in full bloom. Success can skew our view, causing us to believe that we have something that we really don't.

Success can skew our view, causing us to believe that we have something that we really don't.

Wall Street's history supports that. For example, whenever the stock market has plummeted, the pillars of clay that once felt so secure beneath people's feet crumble to the ground, leaving seemingly successful people in despair. When the scales of success fall off our eyes, stark reality begins to set in. The positive side of it is that in these circumstances, many people cry out to God. But just because we cry out to God in desperate times doesn't mean He is the center of our universe. Actually, many times, I have found the opposite to be true.

Take 9/11 for example: When the Twin Towers came crumbling to the ground, the crushing blow dropped America to its knees. People were literally shaken to their core, and they cried out in desperation for God to help them. For a few weeks it felt as if the world slowed down and people from all over our nation began to get right with the Lord out of fear that everything was coming to an end. Thousands of people flooded the altars of our churches; but it didn't take long for the shock to wear off and life to return to "normal," without God.

Putting God Back in Control

We were never created to be a powerless people, subject to the happiness or depression of the environment around us. Rather, our source of wholeness is derived from the author Himself. Only God is the only one who can offer us love and security regardless of our circumstances. Placing God on the throne of our lives is not rocket science, but it does require diligence and taking the right steps.

First Step: Do the Work of Repentance

The very first step to reestablish God on the throne of your life is repentance. The original Greek word for "repent" is *metanoeo*, which means to change the way you think! Repentance roots out inferior and faulty thought processes and replaces them with truth. It's not only necessary to repent for removing God out of His rightful spot in our lives, but we also need to repent for the reasons *why* we displaced Him.

It is so important for us to get to the root issues that have caused the faulty thinking in our hearts. This is where most people miss the bus. They are genuinely sorry for their actions, but because they have no idea what is driving them (what the root issue is), they can't keep their actions and heart in line with their convictions. Therefore, they return once again to their old cycle of thinking.

When I realized that I had put Heather in my "God spot," I had to go back and figure out *why* I had chosen to do that so that I could truly repent.

Second Step: Start the Messy Cleanup

After repentance (changing the way we think), we often have to go back and clean up our mess. For so many of us, there is a huge misconception about what cleaning up our mess really looks like. We have been taught through our childhood experiences that the word "sorry" fixes everything. This couldn't be further from the truth. The word "sorry" doesn't fix anything. I know this because I have three kids! On any given day, it's only a matter of time before one of my children acts out in a "not so fun way" to one of his or her siblings. Usually, it's some sort of short-lived, spur-of-the-moment flair-up about who is going to get the middle seat in the car, or who is going to consume the coveted last GoGurt in the freezer. Kids can always find something to argue about.

It's tempting as a parent to stop the argument as quickly as possible and with exerting the least amount of effort; the goal is to restore chaos to a manageable level. In our efforts to restore order, it is really easy to say something like this: "Kids, knock it off! Elijah, tell your sister you're sorry for being rude to her, or you can go spend the rest of the day in your room!" Now, I'm as guilty as anybody else when it comes to statements like that. However, the problem with just telling my kids what to do and what to say is that it's not really coming from their own hearts. Therefore, any apology they offer is never genuine enough to change their behavior, so the problem still exists.

If our kids are going to change their behavior, they need to be able to figure out why they choose to be disrespectful and then they must want to choose a different behavior so that their "sorry" is productive.

It's no different for you and me; the goal of repentance is not to simply say the words "I'm sorry," but rather to find the root of the issue so that we can fix the behavior.

Third Step: Think Differently

There are a lot of situations in life that seem hard to overcome because of the level of bravery it takes to actually acknowledge there is a problem. We have all met people with the proverbial pet elephant standing in their living room. These people are oblivious to the elephant—their internal world—but usually are quick to point out the elephant standing in other people's living rooms.

To change the metaphor a bit, these people are vampire victims! The victim mentality is one of the deadliest mindsets, because a victim is totally incapable of changing his or her environment. Victims spend massive amounts of time sucking the life out of everyone else because they live in a powerless state of mind. Victims believe that their external world has to change in order for them to be okay. Because a victim is so out of control internally, he or she feels an enormous need to control everyone else.

Powerlessness is the process of giving away ownership and empowering someone or something else as your sole decision maker. You cannot fix something for which you are unwilling to take ownership. It's simply impossible. Taking ownership for your decisions and your problems is the only way to ever become a healthy person. Regardless of what you have come to believe, you are responsible for your own life and actions. When you give up that right to someone else, you have rendered yourself powerless.

Recently, I counseled a couple who typified the victim mentality. Their cry for help came in the form of a Facebook chat. I sat down with my friend Jim and began to assess what was going on. It didn't take him long to explain to me that his wife, Sarah, was impossible to please. She was a black hole that nothing could ever fill; and worse yet, she was a nag. She had no respect for his boundaries, especially when their discussions morphed into arguments. This usually resulted in Jim punching holes in the wall or smashing things.

"She won't let me leave the room or give me time to think; she just keeps hounding me," Jim complained. "Sarah totally controls me!"

My first thought was, *Wowza! I'm so glad I'm not in this guy's shoes!* After giving him time to talk and vent, I began to ask him some pointed questions about himself. First I asked what he had done to work on his relationship with his wife.

There was a long pause accompanied with a sigh. "Um, I guess I'm here," he said.

"Okay," I said. "Did you set up this meeting, or did Sarah?" (I already knew the answer to this question, but I really wanted Jim to know the answer for himself.)

"Uh, she did," he admitted.

Continuing down that train of thought, I said, "Who have you gone to in order to get some help with your relationship?"

Thinking for a second, Jim responded, "Well, I talk to my mom sometimes. Actually, my mom found out because Sarah called her. She normally calls my parents when we are hard at it."

At this point, I was starting to see a pattern in Jim's life. As the questions continued, I found out that Jim didn't talk to anyone about his marriage, including his best friend. To make matters worse, when I asked him what he does to get rid of his pain and frustration, his response was, "I normally just try to forget about it."

It wouldn't take a psychiatrist to figure out that Jim's plan of ignoring his frustration and stuffing his pain wasn't working! This man was punching holes in the wall and turning over tables in the house.

"Jim, it doesn't seem like your plan has been working very well," I said. "What have you done to meet your wife's love languages?" (I was referring to Dr. Gary Chapman's research on the five primary ways people express and interpret love—Words of Affirmation, Quality Time, Receiving Gifts, Acts of Service, and Physical Touch.)

Annoyed, Jim replied, "Even if I try, I don't ever seem to be able to meet them. I've felt really frustrated lately trying to meet Sarah's needs. It feels pretty hopeless." You could hear in his tone of voice the irritation he was carrying inside.

> JIM'S PLAN OF IGNORING HIS FRUSTRATION
> AND STUFFING HIS PAIN WASN'T WORKING.
> THIS MAN WAS PUNCHING HOLES IN THE WALL
> AND TURNING OVER TABLES IN THE HOUSE.

"Jim, what are you going to do about your marriage?"

"I don't know. I wish Sarah wasn't such a mess and so hard to live with," he said.

It was time for me to give some feedback. "Jim, it doesn't feel like she is really the whole problem. You have made her responsible for getting help for you guys. She is the one who is contacting your parents and me. You haven't done anything proactive to work on your relationship other than the things she hounds you about; and you have no process for dealing with the pain and frustration you feel from not being successful. And finally, you still believe that she is the sole problem in this relationship. I'm not surprised that she nags you, Jim. It's the only way that you have ever become motivated in this relationship. You have empowered her to be your mother."

I could see the light bulb exploding in his brain. For the first time in a long while, Jim was beginning to realize that he had given his power away to his wife. She had become responsible for the health of their relationship. As long as he kept this belief system, he would always be powerless to fix what was going on inside of him.

So many people are like Jim. They create a belief system that tells them they are not responsible for the condition of their own life. It is less painful to believe that their problems are everyone else's fault.

SO MANY PEOPLE CREATE A BELIEF SYSTEM
THAT TELLS THEM THEY ARE NOT RESPONSIBLE
FOR THE CONDITION OF THEIR OWN LIFE. IT IS
LESS PAINFUL TO BELIEVE THAT THEIR
PROBLEMS ARE EVERYONE ELSE'S FAULT.

When I first talked with Jim, he had given up on his relationship. He told his wife that he was considering getting a divorce because she was making him miserable. What Jim didn't realize was that if he spent less time worrying about what Sarah was going to do and more time trying to figure out what he was going to do, he could actually fix a majority of his problems. However, Jim had never taken personal responsibility for his life and marriage, so he was always frustrated and overwhelmed because his peace and happiness were at the mercy of his wife.

Once Jim realized he had given all of his power away, he was then able to repent for his victim mentality and figure out what he was going to do to get his power back and love his wife. Today, Jim is no longer a victim, and his marriage is flourishing!

I have always said that any time a problem is 100 percent my fault, it's a good day! I can fix anything that is my fault, but I can't fix anything I don't control.

The day that you take ownership for your life is the day that you begin to take control again.

Fourth Step: Set Healthy Boundaries

One of the major aspects of being in control of your life is the ability to set healthy boundaries with people. Proverbs 25:28 says, "Like a city whose walls are broken down is a man who lacks self-control." The person who lacks the ability to set boundaries will end up being like a broken-down, pillaged city. A defenseless city gets plundered and has nothing of value left to offer anyone.

Personal boundaries are like the protective walls of an ancient city. The purpose of having good boundaries is to protect and nourish yourself so that you can cultivate healthy relationships with others. Without the ability to protect yourself, you have no way to provide protection for anyone else in your life.

A person establishes healthy boundaries through the process of defining his or her virtues, values and needs, and then communicating them to the people that he or she is in relationship with.

When you articulate your boundaries to people, they have the opportunity to respect your needs and virtues and protect your relationship with them. And when they value and protect the things that are important to you, the relationship flourishes. This is the process that builds trust between you and others.

Another great aspect of boundaries is the ability to let people know what you can do/will do and can't do/won't do. You actually have the right and the ability to set limits with others for the health of the relationship. There are no healthy relationships without healthy boundaries.

One of the things we all need to keep in mind when we are setting boundaries is that the primary goal should be to build stronger and deeper relationships with people. Yes, boundaries do keep some people out of relationship with us when they refuse to respect those boundaries. But the main goal of telling people what we need and feel is so they can do the things that cultivate a healthy relationship with us, not so that we have a valid reason to scratch them off of our friend list.

Powerful people know what they need and what they are going to do. They are able to set boundaries because they believe that no one else is responsible for them. No matter what the situation, they are still able to be powerful and choose their responses, because no one else but God is in control of their future. When I understood this truth as it related to Heather, it was a turning point in my ability to approach the future with peace. But I still needed to get free from my sense of the injustice of it all.

CHAPTER 4

Justice Served

The day Heather walked out the door of my life, I experienced everything through a haze. Inside, my bleeding heart had been crying out for justice. After all, it wasn't like I was the only one who was carrying the pain of her selfishness. My children's hearts had been shattered into a thousand tiny pieces. Words don't bring any real solace to kids who are watching their mom leave home for good.

What we often forget about sin is that its consequences affect more than just the person who commits it. More often than not, the people who suffer more are those who have little or no responsibility in the matter, especially those we love the most. My kids were no exception. For me, it was easy to imagine myself being able to walk away from this disaster and never have to see Heather and her boyfriend ever again. But I was going to spend the rest of my life raising kids with the person who had hurt me the most. And I was going to have to share my kids with her boyfriend, not to mention the fact that he had destroyed his own family to be with my wife and kids. To me, it seemed as though there was nothing more unjust in this world than the betrayal of a marriage.

A Change of Heart

As the days passed, I began to think and write about what true justice is. I knew that whatever it was, I had to have it for myself and for my kids. My soul ached at the thought of what my children were going through, and the fact that they didn't deserve this, and neither did I. As I started to pursue the truth, I began to realize that justice was much different from what my instincts were telling me.

AS I PURSUED THE TRUTH, I BEGAN TO REALIZE THAT JUSTICE WAS MUCH DIFFERENT FROM WHAT MY INSTINCTS WERE TELLING ME.

I often envisioned myself like a cowboy in an Old West showdown, doling out justice with a six-shooter. There were so many days when I wanted to do whatever it took to get even, yet I knew that two wrongs would never equal a right. And furthermore, if I punished Heather and her boyfriend to get revenge, my actions would be just as selfish as theirs. My kids would ultimately be the ones who would suffer the most from my destructive behavior. What I really needed was a solution that would make this whole situation better. I didn't need to pour gasoline onto this already raging fire.

My entire world seemed to be hanging in the balance of the answers to two questions: *What is true justice? How do I get it?* I began to think about my own failures. I lay awake deep into the night, pondering how my own careless decisions had cost a Man His life. It wasn't something that I had ever planned, nor would I ever do it on purpose again. But the fact is that it was my sin that drove the nails through Jesus' flesh and bones, and it was my selfishness that pierced His side. If that weren't enough, it was my need for acceptance that broke His back with the cat-o'-nine tails.

We are all guilty of His murder, each and every one of us. Because of our inability to live a sinless life, God gave up His only Son to pay for our foolishness and inability to live right.

God originally set up the world so that we could have an amazing relationship with Him. He created us to be His sons and daughters, and He wanted us to live eternally with Him. The only thing that could ever separate us from our rightful place with Jesus was sin. Sin is our archenemy because it devastates our lives and destroys our relationship with God.

Isaiah paints a beautiful picture of what Christ went through to forgive our sins and reconcile us to God:

> Who believes what we've heard and seen? Who would have thought God's saving power would look like this? The servant grew up before God—a scrawny seedling, a scrubby plant in a parched field. There was nothing attractive about him, nothing to cause us to take a second look. He was looked down on and passed over, a man who suffered, who knew pain firsthand. One look at him and people turned away. We looked down on him, thought he was scum. But the fact is, it was our pains he carried—our disfigurements, all the things wrong with us. We thought he brought it on himself, that God was punishing him for his own failures. But it was our sins that did that to him, that ripped and tore and crushed him—our sins! He took the punishment, and that made us whole. Through his bruises we get healed. We're all like sheep who've wandered off and gotten lost. We've all done our own thing, gone our own way. And God has piled all our sins, everything we've done wrong, on him, on him.

He was beaten, he was tortured, but he didn't say a word. Like a lamb taken to be slaughtered and like a sheep being sheared, he took it all in silence. Justice miscarried, and he was led off—and did anyone really know what was happening? He died without a thought for his own welfare, beaten bloody for the sins of my people. They buried him with the wicked, threw him in a grave with a rich man, even though he'd never hurt a soul or said one word that wasn't true.

Still, it's what God had in mind all along, to crush him with pain. The plan was that he give himself as an offering for sin so that he'd see life come from it—life, life, and more life. And God's plan will deeply prosper through him.

Out of that terrible travail of soul, he'll see that it's worth it and be glad he did it. Through what he experienced, my righteous one, my servant, will make many "righteous ones," as he himself carries the burden of their sins. Therefore I'll reward him extravagantly—the best of everything, the highest honors—because he looked death in the face and didn't flinch, because he embraced the company of the lowest. He took on his own shoulders the sin of the many, he took up the cause of all the black sheep (Isaiah 53:1-12, *THE MESSAGE*).

The day that Jesus was crushed for our sins, He revealed the meaning of true justice. Justice was no longer found in revenge, but in forgiveness. Jesus died so that we could be forgiven. Therefore, unforgiveness became an injustice, because a lack of forgiveness nullifies the payment Christ made for us with His own blood.

There really is no justice in a broken life!

This revelation rocked me to the core as I began to change the way I saw my circumstances. When I was in need of forgiveness, Jesus gave it to me! For the first time, I realized that the only way I was ever going to get justice in this relationship was to pray that Heather's family would get what Jesus paid for. And the only way that my kids were going to win in this mess was to have their mom become a whole person. Once I realized the truth, the urge to punish them for their actions began to fade away. I stopped lying awake at night thinking of ways that they could be punished, and I began contending for their health and wellbeing.

THE DAY THAT JESUS WAS CRUSHED FOR OUR SINS, HE REVEALED THE MEANING OF TRUE JUSTICE. JUSTICE WAS NO LONGER FOUND IN REVENGE, BUT IN FORGIVENESS.

Now That's Justice

Over the years, I have worked with literally hundreds of people who have been victims of some sort of violation. In my line of work, it's not uncommon to help someone, on a weekly basis, who has been raped, cheated on, verbally abused, lied to or all of the above. As you can probably imagine, experiencing any one of these things can be terribly damaging. But the most damaging aspect of being violated is when a person moves into the role of the "punisher" in search of justice.

The "punisher" is a hardhearted taskmaster fueled by bitterness and anger. His or her destructive actions have been justified by an overwhelming sense of injustice and a need for recompense. Although the person is not inherently evil, he or she has been deceived into believing that somehow the fruit of revenge is going to be peace. I know this is a hard pill to swallow, especially if you've been wronged, but here's the truth: Regardless of why you've made bitterness and hatred your best friends, if you carry them around long enough, they will eventually eat you from the inside out.

REGARDLESS OF WHY YOU'VE MADE BITTERNESS AND HATRED YOUR BEST FRIENDS, IF YOU CARRY THEM AROUND LONG ENOUGH, THEY WILL EVENTUALLY EAT YOU FROM THE INSIDE OUT.

If you attended Sunday School as a child, you will probably remember the parable in which Jesus explains this principal of forgiveness, and the lack of it. In this parable of the unforgiving servant, recorded in Matthew 18:21-35, Jesus tells of a king who wanted to reconcile his accounts with his servants. As he began, one servant was brought to him who owed him way more than he could ever pay back. When the king realized this, he commanded the servant, his wife and his kids to be sold for payment. When the servant heard this, he threw himself to his knees and begged for mercy, saying, "Lord, have patience with me and I'll repay you all!" In that moment, the king was so moved with compassion that he forgave the servant of all his debt.

Some time later, the same servant went and found one of his fellow servants who owed him just a few dollars. He grabbed the man and took him by the throat, saying, "Pay me what you owe!" His fellow servant fell down at his feet and begged, "Have patience with me, and I will repay you!" The first servant would not, and he had the second servant who owed him money cast into prison.

When this man's fellow servants saw what he had done, they came and told their lord all that had happened. The lord became angry and called this servant back in to see him. "You wicked servant!" he said. "I forgave you all that debt, because you begged me to do so. Shouldn't you also have had mercy on your fellow servant, even as I had mercy on you?" The lord turned the servant over to the jailers to be tortured until he could pay all that he owed the lord.

Don't you wish the parable would end there? But Jesus throws in one last little line that makes this whole story so pertinent: "This is how my heavenly Father will treat each of you unless you forgive your brother from your heart" (Matthew 18:35).

The principle in this parable is profoundly simple: When you've been forgiven more than you could ever possibly repay, you're expected to forgive in the same fashion. In the event that you forget what was so selflessly given to you, your selfishness will find a home for you in the arms of the tormentors.

Because of what Christ did for us on the cross, and because of the ministry that we have been given—to let Him live His nature through us so that others will be drawn to Him, or as Scripture says, "reconciled" to Him—there is no way that you and I can operate as the punisher and live in the kingdom of God. It just doesn't work!

Paul teaches us in 2 Corinthians 5:17 that we are *new creations* in Christ. He goes on to explain to us that God reconciled us to Himself by not counting our sins against us (see v. 19). Then he reminds us that we have been given the ministry of reconciliation (see v. 19). When you break this passage down, you begin to realize that our ministry as believers in Christ is not to convince the world of their sin. Rather, we are to help reconcile the world back to Christ by not holding people's sins against them. The justice that we need when we have been wronged will be given to us as we help reconcile the world to Jesus!

There is no justice in a broken life. True justice is only found when each person gets what Christ paid for on the cross.

CHAPTER 5

The *Fruit* of *Hard Times*

So often the beautiful things of life are hidden just beyond our breaking point. The fact that you're reading this book tells me that you probably understand some of what I'm talking about. There is a blessing for us when we press through hard times, because the road to wholeness leads down the path of perseverance. It's crucial to have the right mindset in trying times so that we can emerge victorious on the other side of trials.

Our culture's expectation of instant gratification in this information age has robbed us of the understanding of the blessing of perseverance and the lessons of sowing and reaping. So let's focus for a few pages on two vastly different viewpoints of life that represent either the path to a blessed future or a path to always struggling to find a better day.

Let's see if we can unearth the treasures that are so necessary to wholeness and blessing in our personal lives. The principles in this chapter are what helped me get past my painful situation and receive the promise that trials are supposed to yield.

Consider the Farmer

The pain of plowing! But, oh, the reward of reaping! Broken blisters cover the farmer's hands as he works to break up the heat-baked ground. He is beaten down by the scorching sun, and there is no escape from the hot dusty air that his labor is producing. He works tirelessly from dawn till dusk, day in and day out, to produce something that he won't be able to enjoy for months to come. The work is endlessly tiring and grueling. For him, breaking the hard ground is only the first part in this long process of sowing seed.

It is the fruit of the hard times that will carry him through the good times. The fruit he produces in toil will actually create the enjoyable seasons of his near future. The farmer understands this principle; he knows it because this core value has been passed down to him through his forebears. He is not worried about the heavy price he is paying now, nor is he concerned that the seed will not grow. He is diligent in his work, knowing full well that what he plants today will grow tomorrow. Former generations have handed him the faith from which he operates. Experience has given him the confidence to labor, knowing that it will not be in vain.

Not all men have the foresight of the farmer when they are dealing with life's hardships. But without it, you will end up bankrupt, like the lazy man. Let's take a look at the lifestyle of the man who doesn't understand the principle of sowing now to reap later.

The Lazy Man

The lazy man lacks vision. He does not have generations of wisdom to fall back on. He sleeps during the heat of the day because he believes that the only thing a hard day's work in the sun produces is blisters and heatstroke. He has no expectancy of good times or abundance in the future; in fact, he is not concerned about the future because he is too busy trying to survive today while exerting the least amount of effort possible. This man has not been taught the secret of the hard times; he only knows of the punishment that hard labor dishes out.

His view of the world justifies his lifestyle; to him it is better to beg through the winter than to sacrifice in the spring. A man with this mentality will never be full. He walks around in a state of spiritual and emotional anemia, dying to get what others have. Crisis follows him around like collectors chase debt. I am not talking about the hungry who are sowing from what they are getting; I am talking about the habitual taker who has no vision for sowing. To be honest, many of us have an area in our lives that is like the lazy man's view. It may not represent our whole life, but one area.

TO BE HONEST, MANY OF US HAVE AN AREA IN OUR LIVES THAT IS LIKE THE LAZY MAN'S VIEW. IT MAY NOT REPRESENT OUR WHOLE LIFE, BUT ONE AREA.

The "poverty mentality" has plagued the minds of our generation. This often operates like a hereditary disease that has been passed down through the family line. From generation to generation, it holds entire bloodlines depressed and unable to reach their full potential. The poverty mentality says, "There is never enough. No matter what I do I'm always going to be like this." It also says things like, "If only I had a hand up like everyone else in this world, I would make something of myself." This jaded mentality is a prison of hopelessness. Once it has fully set in, its victims will be completely unmotivated and without vision.

Taking the Long View

Let's talk about the farmer once again and look at his view of life. I believe that in doing so, we can glean some practical steps to overcome the poverty mindset and help us grab hold of the fruit of the hard times.

Step 1: Sow with Tears of Joy!

Psalm 126:5 says, "Those who sow in tears shall reap in joy" (*NKJV*). This Scripture paints a picture of what happens when a farmer plants in a hard season. During the agricultural age, if the rains failed to come and the crops ceased to grow, the year's harvest would be meager at best. Often there would not be enough seed from the previous year's harvest to plant a full crop and feed the family. Therefore, the farmer and his family were stuck in a dilemma: should they eat the seed they needed to plant, and avoid starvation for the time being? Or should they go without food and plant the seed in order to have a harvest for the next year?

THE REASON THIS FARMER WAS SOWING SEED WITH TEARS OF JOY WAS BECAUSE AS HE PLANTED THE SEED, HE WAS SEEING BOTH HIS FAMILY'S HUNGER AND THE CROP THAT WOULD BREAK THE POVERTY CYCLE.

Without vision, this farmer would give way to the yearning in his stomach and eat his way into poverty! You can tell from this passage that the farmer had a longer-range vision. The reason this farmer was sowing seed with tears of joy was because as he planted the seed, he was seeing both his family's hunger and the crop that would break the poverty cycle.

Some people are stuck in a perpetual downward spiral of life. Their daily focus has been slowly turned from making a difference in the world to avoiding starvation. This is an easy mentality to fall into.

Laziness (lack of vision) can creep into all areas of life, slowly creating complacency. Without vision you will settle for a hot meal at the end of the day instead of a planted field that will eventually yield a plentiful harvest. Success will be whittled down to a full belly and a warm bed at night. Because you have sown no seed, there is no harvest for the future. You've eaten every bit of your seed to preserve your life now.

If you want to break this cycle, you will have to understand this principle: *In the present you will always have to sacrifice to have a brighter future.*

Step: 2 Today Is the Day!

Benjamin Franklin said, "Never leave something for tomorrow that you can accomplish today." Today is the day. There will never be another today, and each day is a gift from God that will never be given again.

There's something beneficial that happens when you are diligent with the time and the tasks that you have been given. When you have accomplished today the things that were supposed to get done, you have effectively set yourself up for success in more than one way. The first way is that it actually creates momentum in your life. Momentum is the driving force that makes average seem exceptional and common seem profound. I witness this effect all the time in my environment. Someone without momentum in his life will get up on stage and share revelation he has had, and usually a few people will be impacted. In the same fashion, a person with momentum will get up and share a similar revelation and the effect on the crowd is dramatically increased. Why? Because momentum equals favor!

However, there is an opposite effect for the person who does not accomplish tasks when they are given. Even if you accomplish the task a day late, in your mind you know that you should have done it the day before. Therefore, instead of creating momentum and feeling successful when the task is completed, the delay creates a thought process that says you're behind and catching up, instead of that you're ahead and taking over. A lifestyle of catching up creates a sense of hopelessness and low self-esteem.

Another way this principle creates success is called reaping and sowing! In the book of Matthew, Jesus shares a parable of a master who was leaving his home to go on a journey. Before he left, he entrusted his property to his servants. One servant received five talents (money), the second two talents, and the third one talent, according to their respective abilities. After a while, the master returned and asked each servant to give an account of his investment. The first two servants each explained that they put their money to work and doubled it for the master. But the last servant didn't do as good a job with what he had been given. In fact, he explained to the master that he had buried it in a hole, knowing that the master was a hard and unpleasant man.

Long story short is that the master condemned the servant, calling him wicked and lazy; then the master took the one talent and gave it to the servant who had increased what he had been given. But the most powerful part of this whole parable is what Jesus says at the end: "For everyone who has will be given more, and he will have an abundance. Whoever does not have, even what he has will be taken from him" (Mathew 25:29). At first glance, those last few words seem rather harsh. But what

Jesus is really saying is that there is a blessing for each person who is a good steward of what he's been given, regardless of whether it's large or small.

No matter where you are today, you have an opportunity to take what you've been given and grow it. I actually believe that people's greatest challenge is not laziness, or lack of vision, but rather that they have no idea what to do next. The first step in taking ground today is to stop and ask yourself what is hindering you from becoming whole. What is holding you back from God's original plan for your life?

THE FIRST STEP IN TAKING GROUND
TODAY IS TO STOP AND ASK YOURSELF WHAT IS
HINDERING YOU FROM BECOMING WHOLE.

I recently sat in on a training session that taught about the importance of time management. Now, I'm about as excited about time management as the Eskimos are about global warming. I have actually had to learn how to love my calendar. Needless to say, it's been a slow and painful process. But in that meeting the other day, we were learning about the benefit of prioritizing our lives and our calendars by importance rather than letting our schedules be dictated by worthless demands.

Most of the time we get caught up in attending to needs that have no effect or benefit on our future. For example, I can't tell you how many times I've talked to people who have major boundary issues in their life, and yet they have never read a book, listened to a CD, gone to a counselor or even spent any amount of time trying to actually fix their problem. Those same people spend countless hours watching HGTV, reading *Sports Illustrated* magazines and following TV episodes of *24*, like God Himself wrote them. In general, we spend very little time actually focusing and working on the things that will bring us the most return. Therefore, the average person has no idea how to change and grow, because he or she spends very little time focusing on it.

When I first became a father, I can remember how powerless I felt against the demands of my two-year-old. My son had a way of pushing buttons that I didn't even know I had. On several occasions, I can remember walking away from an event or a conversation more frustrated at the fact that my son found flaws in me that no other human being on this entire planet had ever found. It didn't take me too long to realize that my son is a genius, and I was in way over my head! The weeks following this realization consisted of me sitting down every night after the kids went to bed and listening to a course called "Love and Logic" while taking notes. I actually spent several hours each day working on parenting principles and then applying them the very next day.

Most parents, on some level, have felt this way. But what I found throughout all the years of counseling I've done is that most people, even when they identify the problem, don't do anything about it. The Matthew 25 parable addresses this very issue. Since God has entrusted me with three beautiful kids, His expectation for me is that I'm going to be a good steward of what He's given me. When I diligently take care of my kids, my inheritance grows. To be completely honest, when I first started to learn how to parent my kids, I wasn't very good at it. But because I never gave up, and I practiced being a good steward of what He gave me, the Lord has blessed my diligence and entrusted me with the lives of thousands of people.

The farmer's mentality says that there's only one today, and what you do with it will be the result of tomorrow. If you're unhappy with where you're at today, it is because of what you did with your yesterday. Look at each day as a gift, regardless of how tough or how easy the day is. If you sow in tears today, you will reap in joy tomorrow. So wake up from your slumber, wipe the sleep from your eyes and live well today!

IF YOU SOW IN TEARS TODAY, YOU WILL REAP IN JOY TOMORROW. SO WAKE UP FROM YOUR SLUMBER, WIPE THE SLEEP FROM YOUR EYES AND LIVE WELL TODAY!

Step 3: The Joy of Trials!

James 1:2-4 says, "Consider it pure joy, my brothers, whenever you face trials of many kinds, because you know that the testing of your faith develops perseverance. Perseverance must finish its work so that you may be mature and complete, not lacking anything." Here lies one of the greatest secrets to joy in the entire Bible. Yet, upon first glance, this seems like the most ridiculous passage!

I'm not sure how you operate, but the last time I was in a major trial, my first reaction was not to feel hilariously excited about it. I actually didn't think to myself, *I think this trial is going to test my faith so that I'm not going to ever lack a thing.* Instead, my first reaction was to figure out how in the world I got into it so that I could get out of it as quickly as possible!

God's process for creating wholeness in us is through trials that strengthen our faith in Him. The only way we could possibly go through a trial and be super happy about it is if we truly believe that God causes everything (including the hard situations) to work together for good in our lives (see Romans 8:28). I know this doesn't sound like very much fun, but it happens to be true.

There is a great opportunity that comes with every hard season for those who have eyes to see it. So put the farmer's mentality into action and begin the work. There is an excitement that comes for the farmer in every season. He is not thrilled about his blisters, but he is excited about what the pain produces.

I have heard it said many times that adversity pushes a great man to the top. The resistance of hard ground produces strength in the farmer. This strength will carry him all through his life; it will be the strength he will use in his later years. The wisdom that he gained through the labor will be passed down through his family line. His faith will become their faith in their tough seasons; his sons will use his testimony to produce a harvest in their lives, and there will always be enough.

Lessons from the Life of David

I love the life of David. David was a master at being in hard seasons of life and refusing to leave his circumstances until God promoted him. David continuously used adversity as a battering ram to force his way into his destiny.

David's first victories over the lion and the bear strategically set him up for his victory over Goliath, which in turn landed him in the palace ministering to King Saul. It wasn't long before David's ministry to Saul was abruptly ended. In fits of rage, King Saul drove David away from his kingdom and forced him to live like a vagabond, hiding in the hills and caves while Saul tried to kill him. This time in David's life would prove to be one of the most strategic advancements toward his destiny as hundreds of outcasts rallied to him in his vulnerability.

Throughout this time, David refused to kill Saul and take over his kingdom, even though the opportunity presented itself on more than one occasion. David understood that prematurely exiting the season God had him in would be like giving birth to a baby at 12 weeks because you're tired of the process. It's a process that brings about maturity in our lives. Ultimately, David became one of the greatest kings in history. And the outcasts who were hiding with him became his mighty men, his protection throughout the rest of his years (read his story in 1 Samuel 17–31).

The Lord uses adversity in our lives for His purposes. He doesn't always deliver us from resistance, because His first concern is not our comfort. God wants us to become like Him— perfect, not lacking anything. Like the farmer, if we skip the process of breaking the hard ground and tilling the soil, the seed that we scatter will not take root but will wither and die under the scorching sun.

I'm assuming that if you're reading this book today, adversity is standing at your doorstep and peering in your window. I have good news for you: God is creating a way for you to be complete, not lacking anything. Your job in this season is to grab hold of hope and not let go! Like the farmer who labors to produce a crop, your joy lies in the hope of the harvest to come.

Don't Lose Hope

The writer of Hebrews said, "Now faith is the substance of things hoped for, the evidence of things not seen" (Hebrews 11:1, *NKJV*). If you only operate out of what can be seen, you will never be able to lay up an inheritance for your future. Without hope, without the ability to believe and trust God, it is impossible to have faith. And without faith it is impossible to access heaven. What you believe in your heart and what you hope for will eventually be made manifest in the natural realm. If you are stuck in a poverty mindset, and if life has run you through its merry-go-round of disappointment, it's time to change what you expect! Solomon wrote, "For as [a man] thinks in his heart, so is he" (Proverbs 23:7, *NKJV*).

IF YOU ARE STUCK IN A POVERTY MINDSET,
AND IF LIFE HAS RUN YOU THROUGH ITS
MERRY-GO-ROUND OF DISAPPOINTMENT,
IT'S TIME TO CHANGE WHAT YOU EXPECT!

The outcome of your hard times will be what thrusts you into your destiny. The harvest you produce in adversity will provide you with fruit that will sustain you in your later years. In fact, what has been sown through the sacrifice of your youth will be passed down and carried throughout the generations.

The next time you enter a difficult season in life, let the plow of perseverance prepare your field of prosperity.

CHAPTER 6

Unlocking the Inner Man

In the previous chapter, I told you a story about a farmer and a lazy man (a man without vision) to illustrate how our approach to the hard times in life affects our future. I also described the parable of the talents (being good stewards of what we've been given). Stories are such a powerful way to distill truth for living.

This next section begins with a modern parable about a heart that is disconnected from its circumstances. This allegory describes many men and women who have spent their whole lives never connecting to their emotions.

The Frozen Heart

Take a walk with me down a long, slender corridor, a place where life has been forgotten. The hardened walls of ice carry no ability in themselves to feel or breathe, for they have been sealed shut from the light of day. As you pass through the corridor, you can see the work of many hands. Carved deep within the walls of ice are the scars of ancient history. Murals from top to bottom tell the stories of incessant abuse and perversion that have plagued this place.

As you continue down the frozen corridor, you come to a set of steel bars and are unable to go any further. Lying on the floor are thousands of words of affirmation and love, all of them worthless—shattered to pieces—while words of hate and rage claw at the door, trying to find their way into the cage. Peering through the steel bars, you see a heart torn and cold from the empty promises of affectionate deceit. Upon seeing the bleeding heart, you begin to beg and plead to be let in. At the top of your lungs you cry out for mercy, but your words only echo off the ice-laden walls. There is no one here to care, no one to hear your plea. Quickly, your pleading turns to torment as you frantically search for the keys that unlock this door, for it won't be long until this cold heart is frozen in time, unable to ever feel again.

As you dig through the shattered words on the floor, your fingers begin to bleed. But it matters not, for somewhere in the wreckage there must be a key . . . a way in. You dig and dig until the concrete floor meets your bleeding fingers, but still there is no way out. In your frustration you scream at the heart, "Who put you here? Who would leave you here to rot in this frozen grave?" Your words carry through the bars, sinking compassion deep into the freezing heart.

At your words, the heart moans aloud, for it hears only the torment of past love. Slowly, the prison bars grow thicker and the temperature drops in the corridor. Quickly you realize that the heart was the one that built this prison. No longer can it allow itself to unlock the steel cage that took so long to fortify. No longer can it risk the torment of hope deferred and love abused.

Time is running out. The corridor is unbearably cold, and soon you'll be like the heart, numb and unable to move. You have to make a decision to stay and risk the possibility of death, or leave what was once vibrant and full of love behind to die. Death is the black face of evil stealing what was never his to take.

You take a deep breath and think about your family—the wife of your youth and your kids who so affectionately cling to you as their father. You try to breathe deeply over and over, but your breathing quickly turns to gasping as you begin to realize that you can feel nothing for your wife and kids. In your terror, you examine your chest to find that your heart is gone. In a panic, you run back up the corridor to the frozen murals of ice, to the place where memories are stored. Looking high and low, you begin to examine each picture in its intricacies. There you are as a young child clinging to your father, grasping for his affirmation, but you were never good enough. You were the son he didn't need. In his lack of love for you, he broke your spirit with his words. His lack of affection was a trapper's snare, punishing your heart for wanting just a taste of consolation.

SOMEWHERE DOWN THE LINE, LIFE BECAME
A ROUTINE OF SLOWLY SHUTTING DOWN.
AFTER ALL, ONE DOESN'T HAVE TO FEEL IN
ORDER TO LIVE, ESPECIALLY WHEN FEELING
IS WORSE THAN DYING.

Looking through the ice, you begin to realize that your whole life was a horror of memories . . . a testimony of what happens to a heart that is left open to feel. But somewhere down the line, life became a routine of slowly shutting down. After all, one doesn't have to feel in order to live, especially when feeling is worse than dying. You feel like crying, but there are no tears, you're too cold; you're trapped inside yourself, inside the fortress you made.

Running back to the heart, you pound on the cage, screaming to be let in. "Can't you see we're going to die down here?" you shout. The heart groans at your words but is unwilling to move. Falling to your knees, you begin to plead with it, reciting memories of your childhood. "I was there when love was abused, when all you wanted was the touch of a father. I was there when perversion became the comfort for a broken spirit . . . the only way out. I saw the pain in shutting down, knowing that it meant losing the possibility to ever bond again. And I see the hatred that you have toward me for not being able to protect you . . . for not being able to see through the deceptive lies."

For the first time in ages, the heart begins to cry at the re-alization that there's someone who cares—someone who sees where it has been. For even though the heart lives inside of you, it is very much its own person, needing to be explored and un-derstood. The tears pour, and the ice slowly melts as the heart begins to feel again. Never before has the heart felt protected enough to unlock the steel cage, but one by one the bolts be-gin to break as promises are made. "I promise to love you more than anyone else. I promise to find a way to protect you. I prom-ise not to be afraid to feel even when it hurts. And I promise to never disconnect from you again, leaving you alone to fend for yourself!"

Leaving the corridor that day, the only thing that is going to change inside of you is the decision to be powerful and not hide anymore.

MANY OF US HAVE SPENT OUR ENTIRE
LIVES NOT REALIZING WHAT OUR HEART IS
REALLY NEEDING OR EVEN BEING AWARE OF THE
PUNISHMENT THAT LIFE HAS DISHED OUT.

Many of us have spent our entire lives not realizing what our heart is really needing or even being aware of the punishment that life has dished out. Without the ability to connect to our heart, we have no way of meeting our deepest needs. This type of living leaves us desperate for a way to cope with the on-slaught of normal life, because a need unmet leads to pain!

The Defensive Walls of Protection

No one ever begins life with the intent of locking himself or herself inside a prison of ice. After all, who wants to be un-known and alone? The process of shutting down is the body's last-ditch effort at surviving what it deems as blunt-force trauma. When the trauma fails to subside, the mind has to make a decision to either go completely insane or disconnect from the emotional side of reality.

A few years ago, I was introduced to a guy named Blake, who at that time was the only person I had ever met who was among the "living dead." Before I found out anything about him, he asked if I would sit down and help him work through some stuff. As Blake began to share that day, my eyes were opened to a world I'd never seen before.

Blake's early childhood memories were riddled with abuse; most of it intentionally inflicted by the ones who were sup-posed to love him the most. Blake explained to me that at the age of five, he had decided to not feel anymore. He believed that the only people who weren't hurting were people in heaven or people who didn't feel anything!

Blake "lived" for 14 years emotionally shut off and numb from what his heart was feeling. In fact, he said that if you saw him on the street and tried to beat him up, he wouldn't have even protected himself. He explained to me that people who protect themselves have something of value, and if you have something valuable, then you have something to lose. If you have something to lose, then you can feel pain! Blake had fortified his entire heart and emotions inside of a steel cage covered in ice. No words or feelings could get in, and he could feel nothing as long as the bars were in place. He was among the living dead, walking around literally not allowing himself to feel or care about anything in life.

I spent several weeks with Blake, chipping away at the ice-laden walls and removing the bars he had spent a lifetime building. Much like the allegory in this chapter, he was slowly able to create a place where his heart was able to feel again. What I learned was that no one is too far gone, and that Blake is not an isolated case.

There is a large portion of our society that has in some way decided to shut down their emotions. In fact, I've found that most people who shut down didn't necessarily live in a crazy home or endure a ton of abuse. But because they didn't know how to deal with pain, they had to lock up some part of their heart to stay alive.

An Overprotected Heart

I was talking with a friend in her mid-30s about falling in love. To give you some perspective, this girl is top-notch, drop-dead gorgeous and single. Over the past year, I have tried and tried to help her find a mate. Yet no matter what her friends tried to do to help her, she had this idealistic view on how a romantic relationship had to happen, and she was unwilling to budge from that view.

She just knew that the only way a relationship would work for her was for it to be designed by Walt Disney himself. Well, over the course of the year, she began to have a revelation. Through the consolation of many friends, she finally realized that her view on finding a man was actually sabotaging her relationships. She had purposely created an impossible list of things she needed from a husband so that she could protect herself from ever having to risk falling in love *again*.

Obviously, her past relationships had taught her lessons about love that she didn't want to experience again. But because she didn't know how to protect her heart and work through the pain of a broken relationship, her heart did the only thing that it knew to do. It created a way to keep love out.

The most common reason I've found that people shut down is because of their childhood upbringing. As a young child, you're the most vulnerable that you will ever be to the environment around you; and you're the most powerless to change it. Because of this, kids often become victims of their parents' dysfunction. They learn lessons about love and vulnerability that teach them to hide at all costs.

The allegory with which I opened this chapter is a great example of what happens when a man looks back on his childhood and realizes that he was never really loved and cared for. He begins to understand why his heart had to lock itself up in a steel cage. Because this usually happens at a young age, it's common to not even realize what actually happened . . . how your heart actually shut itself down to survive in a frozen environment.

Dysfunction develops in a world where needs go unmet and pain becomes a customary part of your daily diet. When love is given and received on a conditional basis—I'll love you only if you say or do the right things—behaviors such as codependency and control become the norm. These behavioral issues manifest themselves in all kinds of ways, from rage to manipulation to even passivity. Although these people live as if they have no needs, they become masters at filling everyone else's. On the outside, they look like Jesus: running around making sure everyone is taken care of. But in reality, they have learned that having needs and requiring something in a relationship only leads to pain, because that's what they were taught as a child. Therefore, having no needs is an effective but incredibly dysfunctional way to protect them from pain.

The Beauty of Emotion

There are literally hundreds of ways that people protect themselves from having to feel, and there are dozens of ways they compensate for the pain in their lives. But the important thing to realize is that God was the one who designed us with feelings. When God created people, He created us as a masterpiece of emotions. In the purest form, our emotions are motivators. Without them we wouldn't really accomplish much. Emotions are felt in our body and are used to move us to action. When stimulated, our muscles have the ability to tense or relax, and blood vessels dilate or contract depending on the feelings that are coursing through our body. Therefore, our emotions play a big part in motivating to or deterring us from action.

On another level, emotions assist us in making decisions. For example, when we think about something that contradicts our values, our emotions will let us know that it's probably not a good idea. Even just imagining such a scenario can stimulate our emotions to let us know if it feels like a good plan or not.

Without the ability to feel emotions, you are unable to connect to the world around you. Your emotions create strong bonds of connectivity and harmony between you and your social environment. I can't count how many times I've talked with young kids who are completely heartbroken that their parents have never told them the words "I love you." Even as an adult, the pain of living your whole life without having your parents ever emotionally connect to you is incredibly damaging. In contrast, if you look back at some of the best times in your life with your friends or family, it was probably a time when you felt emotionally connected to them. On the most fundamental level, we are created to connect to the world around us on a heart-to-heart level.

> ON THE MOST FUNDAMENTAL LEVEL, WE ARE
> CREATED TO CONNECT TO THE WORLD AROUND
> US ON A HEART-TO-HEART LEVEL.

It is important to remember that God created both positive and negative emotions, and each one of them plays a vital part in our lives. Negative emotions help to keep us alive. They signal warnings and prompt us to act—from running away to avoiding others or even fighting back. Positive emotions are so important because they actually do things like boost our immune system, promote good self-esteem and ward off depression. There are entire books written on this subject alone.

The basic thing to understand is that it was God's original intent that we would live connected to our hearts.

Hello Self

When was the last time you stopped and asked yourself, *How is my heart doing today? What do I need in order to feel okay? Why do I feel the way that I do? What can I do about it?* Your head and your heart are your two best advocates for creating a healthy life. Without the knowledge of what's going on inside of you and what your soul needs, you really have no way of fully taking care of yourself.

Most of us were never taught how to listen to our head and our heart. In fact, many of us were taught lies like, "pain is weakness leaving the body," or "what doesn't kill you only makes you stronger." The truth is that pain is a need begging to be met. The longer a person lives in pain, the more likely it is that his or her heart will shut down. See, most of us don't even know who we are, because we haven't stopped long enough to say hello to ourselves or ask ourselves, "How can I help you?" If we don't know who we are or how we are doing, how can we really share ourselves with others?

It's tempting to avoid asking yourself questions such as "How am I doing?" because sometimes this type of question can lead to you feeling powerless if you don't know what to do about how you're feeling. In the next chapter, you'll learn the truth about pain and how to process through it in a healthy way. No longer will you have to live numb to the world around you or disconnect from your heart. You will learn how to unlock your inner self and break the damaging vows that have kept you trapped inside of yourself.

CHAPTER 7

In the *Comfort* of *Your Own Pain*

Sit for a while with me; kick off your shoes, close your eyes and relax. Welcome to the cold weather of reality, a place that's uncomfortably painful for most of us. I promise not to leave you here too long, as I have once been here too. In the last chapter we talked about your inner self, and all the different ways that it has tried to protect you from the onslaught of a painful reality. In this chapter, you are going to find out that reality is the only safe place to be.

In all of the stories in the previous chapter there is a common denominator, a common theme. None of the people described had a great process for dealing with pain. If you think about it, when was the last time someone taught you how to process through pain? If you are like most people, the answer is probably never. So my next question is, "What did you do with your pain?" Stop reading for a second and actually ask yourself that question. The answer is probably a huge key to unlocking why you are the way you are.

Buried Alive

I remember one particular counseling appointment when I was working with a guy who had just returned from Iraq. Joe was a nurse in the Army, so on a regular basis he was exposed to horrific scenes of mortality. He was in my office because he couldn't feel anymore; he was numb to the world around him. Sitting across from me, I had him close his eyes while I asked him, "Where did you put your emotions?" He sat there for a while before he opened his eyes and described a devastating scene. Here is Joe's account in his own words.

I gotta dig faster! I said to myself, as if there was anyone in the field to hear me. The dirt is very cold and hard to dig a hole in, but I have begun to make some progress. The hole is about two feet deep now; I can just make out the bottom in the dim moonlight. I can hear the men somewhere in the distance shouting and crashing through the brush; they are getting closer but still there's time.

I am covered head to toe in blood and in the freezing mud. I shout to the moon, almost in a wail, "I need to bury this thing before they catch me!" The dirt and rocks have worn down my fingernails until they bleed and burn like fire. I can hear horses drawing close, the hounds are leading them straight to me! Just a few more seconds and I can shove this flesh into the hole, and no one will ever know what I did with it.

I squat just above the hole and look around like some wild animal being hunted. I can hear the hunters now. Their shouts are very close and I can see their lights illuminating the ground around me. With my task almost complete, I pay them nothing more than a fleeting glance. I think to myself for a moment about my bare feet, the footprints I am leaving. They are an open invitation for anyone to dig up what I have so hastily buried, but I can't do anything about it now. I don't have the time.

I cram it into the hole; I shove the loose dirt and rocks back into the cavern that I have made just as a flashlight finds me. A man screams to his friends, "There he is, we have him now!" I dart off into the night running swiftly like a bird cuts through the air. It's buried. I hope they will forget what I have put there. I pray they follow me far away. I leap into a run. I drag my blood-stained body over fallen tree trunks, I dash through creeks; the searing cold water burns for a few short seconds. I can't worry about that now. My bare feet slap the ground hard, shaking me to my core. My feet are ripped to pieces and scream with agony at my every step, but I won't stop running. I quickly make my way down a trail into the valley below; the farmlands look so far away in the moonlight. My very desperate and abrupt exit has left the posse in utter confusion. It will take them a few minutes to regroup. I find peace in this thought.

I break through a thicket of oak trees at the bottom of the trail. On the valley floor, I reach the farmlands. I begin to push my way through the cornfields; they will provide excellent cover and keep the men from finding me quickly. The earth here is soft, hard to make a quick escape and now I know that I am losing ground. I break through the far side of the cornfields where I find an abandoned house. It will provide me a place to rest while they search within the fields. I burst through the front door, closing it behind me. I run to the window that faces the cornfield that I have just come from and open it a crack so I can hear the men when they come for me. Slumping down, I lay my head up against the windowsill for a moment. I don't know how long I was there because I drifted off to sleep.

I awake to a strange orange glow and a crackling sound. Dazed from sleep, I am having trouble comprehending what is happening. It strikes my mind like a lightning bolt that they set the field on fire to flush me out. The smoke is pouring into the house; choking, I run through the living room and pass into the dining room. I smash through the back door and head for the barn. I can't hear much over the roar of the fire. I make it to the barn in a few short seconds. I round the corner; I am trying to make it past the barn and onto another field just beyond. I never saw the man or the axe handle, but it found my head in a perfect swing.

I awake to find a dozen men around me, still staring in horror at the sight before them. You see, the thing I buried, the flesh that I put into the ground, it wasn't another man's. It was mine! I cut out my own heart; I couldn't bare the burden of the pain that it brought me anymore. Love that I had lost, the things that I have done and seen. I had to be rid of it. Rid of it I am. The posse hunted me because they thought that I had killed someone. The only thing that I killed was my ability to feel, forever. I stand up before them, blood-soaked and freezing. A fat, bald man approaches me. He says feebly, "Son, what have you done to yourself? How are you still alive?" I snicker at his remark. I reply in a tone that could skin a man alive, "There is nothing left for me in that piece of tired flesh. It's all that remains of a life that I want nothing more than to forget." He steps back, unsure of how to respond to me.

I lash out again, "How am I still alive, you ask? It's because of my strong will to live a life free of pain."

They bring in the reporters now; they take pictures with their fancy cameras. They write things down in their white notepads with blue lines. I can already see the picture of me in the morning paper: these men standing around me, looking triumphant. I am soaked in blood, caked and dripping with mud. A large hole is cut just below my left nipple, just the perfect size to squeeze my heart out of. Steam can still be seen pouring out of the hole, signs of a still warm body. I am covered in tattered clothes, no shoes. My face is filthy, and shackles dangle from my wrists and ankles. What a sight I must be for them. They fear me in this state. I am some rabid animal that must be destroyed. I have no feelings now. The thought of a man like this scares them. It won't be easy for them to kill me. I won't make it easy for them.

Joe had buried his emotions in some hole far away, never to be seen again. The daily brutality of war was more than he could possibly handle on his own. And once again, without the ability and the consciousness to process through what his heart was feeling, the only other logical option was to bury it.

Regardless of whether your experiences are like Joe's or like my walk through a destructive divorce, you have to have a plan for your pain. One of the greatest misconceptions people have about pain is that time heals it. They think that somehow if they just forget about it or ignore what they're feeling or what's happened to them, it will all go away. This couldn't be further from the truth! If time healed, people in prison would be the most whole people in the world.

Time is a revealer and an enabler. If you plant a seed in the ground and water it, in time it will grow and reveal its species. If you plant that same seed and never give it water, it will never grow. In the same way, if you go through the process of healing, in time you will be made whole. But if you skip the healing process, you'll be left wondering why you are the way you are.

TIME IS A REVEALER AND AN ENABLER. IF YOU PLANT A SEED IN THE GROUND AND WATER IT, IN TIME IT WILL GROW AND REVEAL ITS SPECIES. IF YOU PLANT THAT SAME SEED AND NEVER GIVE IT WATER, IT WILL NEVER GROW.

Blessed Are Those Who Mourn

Matthew wrote, "Blessed are those who mourn, for they will be comforted" (Matthew 5:4). If what this verse is saying is true, then it could also read, "Cursed are those who don't mourn, for they are not comforted." The actual process of working through pain and becoming a whole person is the process of acknowledging and mourning your pain.

The challenge of this type of thinking is that none of us likes to sit around and think about our emotional pain. Most of the time, pain causes us to feel so incredibly powerless and hopeless that just focusing on it makes it worse. Therefore, the typical response to pain is to ignore it. However, without the process of mourning, there is no comfort!

To mourn pain doesn't mean that you just sit there and think about it until you get really angry and overwhelmed (although this may happen as part of the process). The healthy way to mourn your pain requires a beginning and an end to the process. Just like a funeral, you know that you are going to walk in and experience the life of the person who died through pictures and kind words. You also know that you're probably going to cry at the reality that he or she is gone. But finally, if you have ever experienced a death in the family, you know that the pain eventually goes away after the tears are gone and the memories are processed.

Disarming the Inner Time Bomb

The day that Heather left me, all of the memories and shared experiences that used to bring me warm feelings were instantly transformed into objects of heartache. No longer were the thoughts of my wedding day or our first date happy memories. No longer did it bring me joy to think about our honeymoon night, and the way I'd given her my heart. I was alone, trapped inside of a mind full of memories, each one of them cutting me to the core. As much as I wanted to just wake up and have it all be gone, I was stuck with all of those memories inside of me.

I quickly realized that memories are like time bombs: if I failed to acknowledge their presence and disarm them, they would explode inside of me, creating incredible amounts of uncontrollable anger. If I let the anger out in an unhealthy way, it would hurt the ones I loved the most, my kids.

I began to change the way that I saw my pain. Memories that used to send me crashing were now welcomed in, and I carefully pondered and mourned each one until the sting was gone. This is the practice of stewardship. That's right, you have to steward every painful thought, looking at each one as a gift brought forward to make you whole. Once I overcame the fear of being in pain, and I started to face each memory, I felt an excitement, because every processed memory was a step toward freedom.

ONCE I OVERCAME THE FEAR OF BEING IN PAIN, AND I STARTED TO FACE EACH MEMORY, I FELT AN EXCITEMENT, BECAUSE EVERY PROCESSED MEMORY WAS A STEP TOWARD FREEDOM.

I can remember the first time I thought about my wedding day after Heather had left. I was in the middle of worship during the School of Ministry session, just lying up on stage enjoying God's presence. Almost without warning, I was completely caught up in the memory of my wedding. There she was, riding in on a chocolate brown horse being led by her brother. My heart pounded in my chest as she slowly walked toward me to the soundtrack of the film *Braveheart*. Soon she was at the altar and I was there to take her hand.

The pastor spoke and we took Communion, and in a moment we were back at the altar exchanging vows. There I was, giving her my heart that I so desperately needed back. At her words, the tears began to run and the memory continued to play. The worship from the School of Ministry was pounding in my ears and the thought of her never coming back was dripping down my face.

It wasn't long before I couldn't control myself, and the tears turned to wailing. I quickly realized that worship was going to end in a minute and I was going to be left onstage in a puddle of tears. Leaving worship, I headed upstairs to my office, thinking to myself, *I don't want to lose this memory; I want to work all the way through it.* When I finally reached my office, I quickly turned on some sad music and settled back into the memory.

I sat there that day in my office allowing the memories of my wedding day to play in my head as I cried through the reality that it was really over. I can remember picturing her walking down the aisle over and over again, while I asked God what He wanted me to do with these thoughts. Eventually, the details of our wedding and the reality that it was over didn't hold the same sting as the first time it hit. God began to answer the questions the memories brought to me, questions like "What's going to happen to my kids?" and "Am I ever going to love again?" One by one the memories would come, each one with a different sting. And one by one I would cry through them until the sting was gone and God had answered my questions.

The Pain Doesn't Have to Stay

Throughout the process of working through my pain, I realized that without the ability to connect and feel and let out what was going on in my heart, I would have no way of being free. Most Christians have been so programmed to look only at the positive that it can easily seem like a violation to focus on and mourn their losses.

Recently, I met with a woman for a counseling appointment who said she never cries and she has a hard time expressing her needs to others. The perplexing thing about her is that she is Superwoman in the room, attending to everybody else's needs, making them feel loved and accepted. But when it comes to her, she would rather listen to someone else than express what she is dealing with at that moment.

Sitting in my office that day, Megan began to tell me her story. Her father died when she was really young, leaving her with an incredible amount of pain at a young age. Around the age of 18, she received a phone call that her mother had died in a car accident. She was scared and alone. In one day she had gone from making plans to hang out with her mom to being left alone in this world.

Shortly after her mother died, her friends and family gathered together to attend the funeral. Kind words were spoken and beautiful songs were sung, and soon it was all over and done with. After the funeral, Megan's friends gathered around her and took her into the living room of her house for a time of worship and praise. They felt like she needed to start a new chapter in her life and worship her way out of this terrible time.

The more I listened to Megan that day, the more I realized that she had never allowed herself to mourn the loss of her parents. And because Megan never mourned, she was never free of the pain. Megan's friends had great intentions in wanting her to be free of pain and feel joy and be able to praise. But what they didn't realize is that by not allowing her to mourn her loss and work through the pain, she was stuck with it.

Megan had never allowed herself to access all of her heart, because she believed that the pain would never go away. Therefore, it was pointless to even go there. She was trapped inside the façade of never feeling sad, but only acting happy. In reality, her heart was screaming for someone to acknowledge the pain.

Allowing ourselves to only be happy is as dysfunctional as only allowing ourselves to feel pain. As we learned in the previous chapter, God created every emotion, and each one has a specific purpose.

Megan and I spent a large portion of our time in that counseling appointment facing the reality that her mom and dad were never going to come back. I had her do things like write letters to her mom about how she felt the day she died, and journal about how it felt to get that phone call. Megan began to learn that she is not alone in her pain; God had answers for where she was at and what she needed. Over time, through processing the reality of loss and connecting to her heart, she was able to unlock her tears and face the reality that she so dreaded. To this day, Megan remains free from the pain of not knowing herself and the feeling of being alone in this world.

ALLOWING OURSELVES TO ONLY BE HAPPY IS AS DYSFUNCTIONAL AS ONLY ALLOWING OURSELVES TO FEEL PAIN. GOD CREATED EVERY EMOTION, AND EACH ONE HAS A SPECIFIC PURPOSE

Purging the Pain

With reality often comes the onslaught of emotions that have been all bottled up inside. As I said before, the average Christian will want to dumb down what they're actually feeling because somehow it seems like a sin to have any other thought besides happy ones.

When I started processing through the fact that Heather had left me for another man, I began to have a myriad of emotions, from anger and hatred to sorrow and grief. Often they would manifest in different ways. What I allowed myself to do was to be brutally honest with what I really felt about what had happened to me.

If you remember back to chapter 4, "Justice Served," you know that my heart was for her wellbeing and wholeness. But for myself, I couldn't shove away or hide the fact that I felt terribly wronged and ripped off. I spent several months writing sad songs and strikingly honest letters about what had happened and how I felt, letters that I never sent to her. For weeks

I would wake up every night around three in the morning with poetry going through my head. I gave myself permission to yell, scream or write letters about what she had done and how wrong that was, as long as it wasn't going to hurt anyone else. (Of course, I had to make sure the kids didn't hear me.)

By my being honest with myself about what was going on inside of me, in the privacy of my own home, I was able to purge the emotions I was feeling without hurting anyone else around me. I found that over and over again people who go through tremendous amounts of pain and never let themselves process in the safety of their home usually end up exploding at the wrong time.

BY MY BEING HONEST WITH MYSELF ABOUT
WHAT WAS GOING ON INSIDE OF ME, I WAS ABLE
TO PURGE THE EMOTIONS I WAS FEELING
WITHOUT HURTING ANYONE ELSE AROUND ME.

The emotions I expressed through a song or a poem were not a commentary on how I wanted to feel about Heather or where I was planning on staying forever. Rather, they were snapshots of how I was feeling in that moment. Because I spent a lot of time being honest with myself in the moment and processing it out loud, when I would encounter her in person, I didn't feel an angry bomb inside wanting to explode.

Real Men and Women Cry

We live in a world where our heroes are made of cobalt steel. They are impervious to the natural laws of humanity, able to take on the hordes of hell with only a flaming arrow and leave completely unscathed. These heroes are broadcast before our eyes and printed upon our minds as at the top of the hierarchy of society. Our women adore them and our men are taught to praise their cold-heartedness as badges of honor, wanting to somehow be like them. These men feel no pain, fear no evil and are able to drop a woman like their last bad habit.

As well, many parents have done a fine job of reinforcing this belief system that it's not normal to be vulnerable, and it's especially not okay to show emotion. In many homes, the children's ability to be honest about feelings is incredibly hard because that is not what their parents are modeling. And in most homes, emotions are hidden, like unconfessed sins. This unrealistic view of humanity has contributed heavily to the desensitization of our emotions.

A Child Will Lead Them

Long before you're taught that heroes don't feel pain, and long before you're taught that family members hide their hearts, God taught you how to work through pain. If you've ever watched young children play together, you know it's only a matter of time before the final straw and the crying begins. In my house it often looks like one of the older kids has somehow taken advantage of the younger one. Without even being in the same room as the kids, I can already tell what's happening by the high-pitched wailing that's coming from the other room. Usually it requires my presence in order to resolve the issue at hand. The interesting thing about these interactions is not what happens during the conflict, but what happens after.

My youngest, who can cry so the whole neighborhood can hear him, is back playing happily with the other kids again in only a matter of minutes. How does this happen? If this were a group of adults, the person who has been taken advantage of would need days or weeks to recover. However, children have an inherent ability to work through heartache because they have the right belief system. No one has taught them yet that it's not okay to show emotion; so without even thinking about it, as soon as they feel pain, they begin to cry. Their crying purges them from the emotions of hurt they are feeling in the moment. And once the crying is done, the emotion is dealt with and they get on with life, happy as can be.

Someone once said, "When you cry, you get all caught up," and they were right! What we've been taught through the media and from our parents about crying and being emotional has to change. The man made of cobalt steel is all rusted inside. And the coldhearted Lone Ranger dad is riding his horse into the sunset looking for his heart. God created in us the ability to cry because He knew that we would need a way of purging our pain. If we don't allow ourselves the right to get out what's on the inside, it stays bottled up in our souls and hardens our hearts. If we stay hurt long enough, eventually we will be overcome by bitter lies and vicious vows.

IF WE DON'T ALLOW OURSELVES THE RIGHT TO GET OUT WHAT'S ON THE INSIDE, IT STAYS BOTTLED UP IN OUR SOULS AND HARDENS OUR HEARTS.

Exposing a Harmful Belief System

Lies take form in a world where people are punished for showing emotion or where there is no relief for the pain. Are you numb? Do you walk around wishing you could feel more, but you can't? Do the words "I love you" said out loud send an awkward burn through your body? Or does the thought of sharing your needs with another seem pointless or weak? These are all signs that you're operating under a belief system of lies.

John, the apostle of love, wrote, "There is no fear in love, but perfect love casts out fear. For fear has to do with punishment, and whoever fears has not been perfected in love" (1 John 4:18. *ESV*). If you could pluck the fear out from your belief system, you would quickly find that you have been a puppet on a string, being danced through this life by the master of fear. Your thoughts, words and actions have all been polluted by the fear of punishment or an unfounded lie.

Let me explain. Megan, the woman at the beginning of the chapter whose parents had died, didn't allow herself to cry or have needs. When she told me this, I had her close her eyes, and I asked her to tell me the first thing that popped into her head.

Megan looked up at me and said, "I believe that if I start crying, I won't stop."

Then I asked Megan what she believed to be true about pain. She quickly answered, "That there is no cure for pain." Previous to our conversation, Megan had never consciously thought through the fact that she believed that crying never ends and there is no cure for pain. Megan was living a life bound by fear and controlled by the master of lies. Without uprooting the lies, she would remain imprisoned!

I have found that Christians process so much that we talk ourselves out of what we really believe. But when Megan told me the first thing that popped into her mind when she closed her eyes, I knew what she really believed to be true in her subconscious. One thing we have to understand is that we do not just operate out of our conscious state of mind. Rather, the decisions that we make and the way that we behave are primarily manifestations of our subconscious thought processes.

THE DECISIONS WE MAKE AND THE WAY WE
BEHAVE ARE PRIMARILY MANIFESTATIONS OF
OUR SUBCONSCIOUS THOUGHT PROCESSES.

I remember feeling anxiety one day so dreadfully that I couldn't get it to lift. It was like a bad dream that I had woken up from and couldn't shake. Finally, I got tired of feeling that way and I retreated to my bed for a middle-of-the-day nap, hoping to get some relief from the tension. While lying in bed, I began to ask the Holy Spirit why I felt anxiety. What He said to me was shocking.

He said, "You use anxiety as a tool. You've partnered with it to help you."

Now, I'm not sure about you, but there is no way on God's green earth that I want to make anxiety any type of partner of mine. That would be like making my bed in an alligator nest! So I said to the Holy Spirit, "How did I make anxiety my partner?"

He said, "You wait until the last minute to get things done, until you feel anxiety. Once you feel anxiety, you're motivated to accomplish tasks you have been neglecting." Light bulbs began to go off in my head as He revealed the partnership I had made with anxiety.

Many people have done the same thing with fear. They build partnerships with fear to protect themselves from rejection. Fear has told them things like, "If you try to be yourself, you'll be rejected." Or "The only way to get through this time is to medicate yourself with pornography." Or even deceptions like, "No one else knows how you feel, no one really under-stands you." Lies, like the ones that Megan believed, imprison the soul and make you a powerless puppet of fear.

Discovering the Lie

Perfect love casts out all fear! The most powerful thing that you can do for yourself when you're bound by fear is to allow God's perfect love to come in and be your master. His love literally drives out the lies that have kept you bound and locked up. But first you must find out how you have partnered with fear.

When Megan told me that she believed if she started cry-ing she would never stop, I asked the Holy Spirit to tell her the truth. The Holy Spirit began to reveal to her that if she allowed herself to grieve and feel emotion, she would become whole. We asked the Holy Spirit if He would show her the truth about pain. He showed her that pain was not something that was in-curable, but that it was actually easily taken care of.

When I found out that I'd come into partnership with anx-iety, I had to do the same thing that the Holy Spirit taught Megan. I had to break the covenant that I'd made with fear. This is a simple process of renouncing the lie that you believe to be true and taking on God's truth in place of it.

Taking Action

The important part of all this is that you must realize that while you can renounce lies and break partnerships all day long, if you don't change your actions, you've really done nothing to transform yourself. For example, when I finished the counsel-ing appointment with Megan, I sent her home to connect with her pain and learn how to cry. In doing so, she broke the shack-les of fear that had held her bound for so long.

In my case, the day I found out that anxiety had become my partner, I had a decision to make: *Do I learn to handle things on time, or am I going to procrastinate the way I've always done?* I couldn't break the partnership and keep the same actions I had before. My behavior had to reflect my new belief system.

If you recognize yourself in this chapter, it is the lying tongue of accusation that has kept you locked up in your fear and pain. In order to truly break free, you need to begin to ask yourself some questions and break the partnerships that you have made.

IF YOU RECOGNIZE YOURSELF IN THIS CHAPTER, IT IS THE LYING TONGUE OF ACCUSATION THAT HAS KEPT YOU LOCKED UP IN YOUR FEAR AND PAIN.

If you've never been able to show your emotions, ask yourself what you believe will happen if you show emotion. If you've always been angry, ask yourself what you believe will happen if you put down your anger. If you've never been able to say I love you, ask yourself what you believe will happen if you tell the people around you that you love them. Chances are good that you'll start to find out the truth about why you are the way you are.

Once you've done this and found the lie, it's time to ask the Holy Spirit what the truth is about the lies you believe. Once you have renounced the lies and accepted the truth, it's time to change your thought processes and your daily patterns.

Practice Creates Courage

The most common expectation I've found in the counseling I've done is that people want results in "pill" form. They come in with major life issues and expect me to hand them two magic pills that if taken three times a day will make every problem disappear. Obviously, this isn't even close to how it works. The truth is that the very thing you're afraid of is the thing you're probably going to have to do. The good news is that with practice comes courage!

The key to getting completely well in a particular area is to strengthen yourself in that area. For example, if you have spent your whole life shut down because you're afraid of being rejected and hurt, then I would suggest you read a book on how to set appropriate boundaries, and that you get some teaching on how to communicate your feelings so that you will be on your way to becoming a powerful person in that area. If you have been afraid to cry and process emotion, then I would highly recommend keeping a journal and allowing yourself to sit with God and process through your past pain. Allow Him to answer questions that have carried so much hurt. I even recommend writing letters you never send and poems that only you read to help you process your pain.

The Boundary Lines for Health

One of the most common questions I am asked is, "How often should I process through my pain?" Eventually, a person is going to need to work through every painful or fearful thought and memory because anything he or she is afraid to look at is ultimately going to keep him or her bound. However, processing through pain is a lot like lifting weights. If you lift weights every day, all day long, instead of getting stronger you will actually break down your body to the point where you can't function. If you process through your pain all day long, every day, and never take a break emotionally, you will be on your way to emotional breakdown. You will become so tired and weak that depression may set in.

PROCESSING THROUGH PAIN IS A LOT LIKE
LIFTING WEIGHTS. IF YOU LIFT WEIGHTS EVERY
DAY, ALL DAY LONG, INSTEAD OF GETTING
STRONGER YOU WILL BREAK DOWN YOUR BODY
TO THE POINT WHERE YOU CAN'T FUNCTION.

Any time you find yourself depressed, most likely you believe a lie. Earlier in this chapter I talked about warding off lies. Do you remember chapter 5, where I wrote about the fruit of the hard times? Any time you start to feel hopeless, you need to go back and reread that chapter. Then have your friends remind you about your true destiny and what God says about you. It is also important when you are working through stressful seasons that you eat right, sleep well, exercise and have fun. I've found that most people who have breakdowns failed to take those simple steps.

Let me be clear here, when I'm talking about processing through every thought, I'm specifically referring to events that still cause you pain, not something that's long past healed up and pain free. It's important to remember that pain was never meant to be a lifestyle—something you live with forever. Rather, pain helps you define the problem so that it can be exterminated from your life. Overemphasizing pain can create a martyr complex and become a way of life instead of a tool that points out brokenness so that it can be mended.

Before moving on to the next chapter, take time to really work through any pain you feel in your heart. You have to remind yourself that every painful thought can be a gift that leads you toward wholeness. Through the process of mourning your pain and replacing lies with truth, you walk toward emotional health. In the next chapter, you will see how forgiveness partners with truth to heal our hearts and free our souls.

CHAPTER 8

The *Supernatural Power* of *Forgiveness*

Jody Bell was a beauty queen of sorts. She was young, with smooth brown hair, a great complexion and incredible beauty. So beautiful, in fact, that it became a detriment to her. Having an absent father, and only a distraught mother to fall back on, she became a master at using her physical attributes to draw men in to fill her needs.

One after another the violations came, as her need to feel loved dramatically increased. And with each violation of her conscience came the onslaught of lies. It didn't take long for her party lifestyle to drain the beauty of her innocence away. Like a gift that had to be constantly repackaged, she no longer felt special. She began to see herself through words like "slut" and "whore." She had painted her face red; for now her only true friends were regret and self-hatred, which accompanied her every moment of the day.

The pain of losing herself was unbearable. She hated life, and even more than that, she hated herself. Around the age of 17, she began to cut her arms to express the misery she felt inside. Cutting became a way of life, the only escape for a girl who now hated even her own skin. Her own accusations had all pointed to the fact that she was all used up and no longer worth anything. After all, who would love someone who had carved deep scars into her own arms?

Jody's story is not that uncommon. Although the details may be different, the truth remains the same: *The hardest person to love and forgive is most often yourself.* Perhaps you see yourself in this story or in parts of this story. Your poor decisions have brought you and the ones you love misery. And because it was you that made the decisions, you're the only one to blame. Regret is like a mortal wound that keeps you trapped in the past, slowly bleeding the life from you. Until the wound is completely healed, your future will always be tainted by regret and self-hatred.

REGRET IS LIKE A MORTAL WOUND THAT
KEEPS YOU TRAPPED IN THE PAST,
SLOWLY BLEEDING THE LIFE FROM YOU.
UNTIL THE WOUND IS COMPLETELY HEALED,
YOUR FUTURE WILL ALWAYS BE TAINTED BY
REGRET AND SELF-HATRED.

Guilt and Shame

There are two other emotions that keep close company: guilt and shame. I help oversee a men's sexual purity group for sex addicts. These men come from all walks of life. Some are rich, some are poor; some have had great parents, and some have lived terrible lives. But most of the men who sit in that room are actually heroes of mine. They're the ones who have acknowledged that their problem is much greater than them.

Over the course of nine months, I spent a lot of time teaching them how to break the cycle of destruction in their lives. But there is one night in particular that stands out to me. I was explaining about the power that shame holds over us. Then I had each man close his eyes, and I asked, "How many of you are dealing with shame right now?" This particular night there were probably 45 to 50 men in the room, and every man except for three raised a hand. Then I told those men to ask the Holy Spirit why they had kept shame in their life. After a few minutes of silence, I began to ask each man what the Holy Spirit had shown him.

The first guy who spoke had been free from the bonds of pornography for months, probably even for as much as a year. But prior to coming into this group, he had lost his whole family to his addiction. I asked him what the Holy Spirit had shown him. If he was free of pornography, why did he still have shame in his life?

He sat there for a second and thought before answering sheepishly, "The Holy Spirit showed me that I have kept shame around so that people would think I was really sorry for what I have done. If I walked around the church, the place where people were hurt the most, and I was happy, I believed they would no longer think that I had repented and was sorry for what I had done."

I then proceeded to ask the Holy Spirit to show this man where he had put his identity. Thinking for a second, he said, "It's in my ex-wife's back pocket!" I said, "That's right! If your wife had forgiven you and was happy, you would forgive yourself and be okay with who you are. But because your wife has chosen to live in bitterness, you feel guilty about feeling free and happy, knowing what you've done!"

That night, each man discovered that shame was a façade, a protection they had been using to make the world see them in a certain light. One of the most powerful revelations a guy had that night was that he had used shame to keep him in heaven. He started out by saying, "If I was to go on a trip, the very first thing I would put in my bag would be shame. I can't remember a day that I've ever gone without it."

This particular man was in his forties and had four kids and a beautiful wife. His earliest childhood memories are of sitting in the hallway waiting for his dad to finish his porn so that he could play with him. Obviously, the sins of his father were passed down to him, and like his dad, he had been bound by pornography since his adolescence. I asked, "What do you mean when you say that shame is keeping you in heaven?" He explained that the feeling of shame reminds him every day of how horrible he felt when he looked at pornography. Without the feeling of shame, he believed that he would just go right back to it.

Each of these men learned about the destructive power of shame that night. Even though many of them had been free of pornography for months and had repented and asked for forgiveness, they still carried shame around as though it were a gift to them. In reality, shame is a fiery dart, shot from the devil himself, that has been designed to keep a person bound in his sin. Given an opportunity, shame will mask itself as your best friend, and it will convince you that it's only there to help you. All the while, it's stealing your freedom and raping your identity.

Sin is the devil's hand that disfigures heaven's masterpiece—the human soul—into a broken-down corpse. Satan's lies and accusations are laced with just enough truth that the pill is easy to swallow. But any time you have a thought in your head about you that didn't come from the heart of God, you're trespassing against your own body. Paul said, "For all have sinned and fall short of the glory of God" (Romans 3:23). It was for this purpose that Christ died and gave Himself on the cross, so that we would no longer live bound by the laws of sin but live free in our God-given identity as sons and daughters of the living King!

Regardless of what you have done, the same freedom that was extended to me and set me free will also set you free. When you understand the grace of Christ and what He did for you on the cross, the shackles of guilt and shame are removed, because Christ has already paid for your sin.

To be fully free and whole when you're the one that committed the crime, you have to extend the same forgiveness to yourself that you would extend to someone else, and you have to love yourself into wholeness again. To get to that place, you have to gain the right understanding of repentance; if you don't figure out what the real problem is (your root issues), you'll be constantly stuck in managing a cycle of pain. And without solving the reasons why you don't love yourself, or why you have allowed guilt and shame to rule your life, you can desire to be different all day long, but nothing will change, because the cycle of sin continues to repeat itself.

Moving Toward Repentance and Root Issues

Just the other day, I counseled a guy who was struggling with pornography. He told me that he usually looks at porn about once a month or so. After listening to his story, I simply asked him, "What do you feel like right before you look at porn?" He said, "I feel lonely and out of control."

I began to ask him more questions to figure out where the loneliness and the feeling of being out of control were coming from. So I asked, "What was your childhood like? Tell me about your parents." He explained to me that his dad had left him when he was young, and even though his dad is in his life now, they don't have a deep connection at all. His mom didn't quite know how to handle the divorce, and so in her best efforts to cope, she moved from place to place his whole life. As his past began to unfold before me, it became strikingly clear why he felt lonely and out of control.

The most important people in his life (his mom and dad) were emotionally distant. When he needed them the most, they weren't there to help him. To make matters worse, his mother's inability to settle down created in him a feeling of hopelessness. Living out of boxes and never being able to settle down and plant roots created an incredible feeling of loneliness and instability. As a young child, he had no way of filling his need for intimacy. Therefore, pornography became his escape for feeling powerless and unknown.

Before he came into my office, he thought he had a pornography problem; but when he left my office, he realized that pornography was a symptom of a much greater problem. He had never learned how to get his needs met through healthy relationships.

Shame told him that if he asked someone for help, he'd be looked upon as irresponsible and ultimately be rejected. Now he knew that he needed to repent and change the way he thought about relationships and life. He needed to learn how to get his needs met from God and the community that surrounded him so that he could get free from his cycle of destruction and guilt.

Finding Full Freedom in Forgiveness

Forgiveness is one of the most misunderstood and misused truths in the Kingdom. I have literally met hundreds of people who have spent years trying to forgive people. Although their efforts were genuine and their hearts were right, they continued to struggle with bitterness and offense for years.

Forgiveness does not mean that you have to feel great about what happened to you; nor does it mean that you have to reconcile with the violating party. Neither does it mean that you ever have to trust a person who violates you. Trust and forgiveness are not the same thing. For example, if a woman is raped in a dark alley, she must forgive the rapist, for otherwise hatred and bitterness will eat her from the inside out. But she never has to be alone with that man again. Trust is earned through relationship, but forgiveness was purchased by Christ on the cross.

TRUST AND FORGIVENESS ARE NOT THE SAME THING. TRUST IS EARNED THROUGH RELATIONSHIP, BUT FORGIVENESS WAS PURCHASED BY CHRIST ON THE CROSS.

Extending forgiveness means that you give God permission to get justice on your behalf, and you release people from your judgment and from your attempts to get justice through punishment (we talked about true justice in chapter 4). I've discovered in working with many people that if they ask the Holy Spirit how He sees the violating party, He will give them compassion for that person or persons. Once they feel compassion, applying forgiveness is much easier.

Jesus Was Forsaken So That We Could Be Accepted

When Jesus died on the cross, He didn't put His fingers to His ears and say, "La, la, la, I'm not thinking about You punishing Me." Imagine for a moment how badly Jesus, who'd been at His Father's side throughout eternity past, must have felt at the crucifixion when His Father abandoned Him. He said, "My God, my God, why have you forsaken me?" (Matthew 27:46). For the first time, the eternal Son felt separated from the Father! Jesus, having taken the sin of the whole world upon Himself, experienced the anguish that sin brings, because sin separates us from the Father. The grief of abandonment was worse than the pain of crucifixion!

The Bible says, "They offered Jesus wine to drink, mixed with gall; but after tasting it, he refused to drink it" (Matthew 27:34). Gall may have been a painkiller, while wine was a well-known painkiller. Christ refused the gall and the wine because He didn't want to just die for our sins, but He also wanted our pain to die with Him, and so He refused to numb His suffering. Therefore, living with pain is a violation of the cross. We only embrace pain long enough to discover its root cause and apply the cure. We don't have to be afraid of pain, because it's an enemy that was defeated at Calvary.

WE ONLY EMBRACE PAIN LONG ENOUGH
TO DISCOVER ITS ROOT CAUSE AND APPLY
THE CURE. WE DON'T HAVE TO BE AFRAID
OF PAIN, BECAUSE IT'S AN ENEMY THAT
WAS DEFEATED AT CALVARY.

If you are born again and you are still dealing with something from the past that is causing you pain, refer back to chapters 6 and 7, and work through it. Great freedom comes when we realize all that Christ accomplished for us. Out of that realization, we have compassion for the people who have wronged us. It is in this place that I've found the most victory in my life and in the lives of those around me.

Our Process of Forgiveness

There are many people who haven't taken full advantage of Jesus' finished work on the cross. Consequently, they suffer for themselves instead of experiencing the full power of Christ's redemption. This point was driven home to me again the other night when I ministered to a young lady on the prayer line at our church.

Unbeknownst to me, a young man had taken cruel advantage of her when she was a kid. The second I started to pray for her, I could tell that she didn't love herself. I quietly whispered, "Repeat after me . . . I love myself!" My words caused her to tremble as pain inside of her began to well up. She had been carrying around this torment for years, but it had been suppressed by the lies that bound her.

She reluctantly repeated, "I . . . I . . . I love myself."

Then I said, "Now say, I forgive myself."

With her chin quivering, she repeated the words after me, "I forgive myself."

I then said, "I am fully loved!"

Once again she took a deep breath, trying to control the emotions that were beginning to overwhelm her. "I'm fully loved," she said. I proceeded to walk her through acknowledging her pain. She was fighting hard to keep from feeling the pain buried deep inside of her.

I had her repeat after me, "I renounce the lie that it's not okay to feel pain. I renounce the lie that crying is weakness. I renounce the lie that it's wrong to think about what happened to me." As we got to the last one, I could tell that the pain was completely overwhelming her. Her whole body was shaking, and she was starting to say that she couldn't think about it.

Once again I said to her, "I want you to tell him in your mind how he made you feel when he violated you!" She remained quiet. I could tell that she was beginning to press through her pain because she was getting angry and more emotional as time went by. Suddenly, she burst out yelling on the prayer line, "I hate you, I hate you for what you did to me! I hate you for stealing my innocence and for using peer pressure to trap me!"

She went on like this for a while. Then I said to her, "I want you to ask the Holy Spirit how He sees him."

She paused for a bit to listen to the Holy Spirit, and then she said, "He loves him like He loves me!"

At this point, she began to understand that even though she felt hatred and heartache toward the young man, God loved him like He loved her. After she connected with the pain of her past circumstances and verbalized how destructive his actions were toward her, and asked the Holy Spirit how He saw him, suddenly she felt compassion for him and was ready for the next step.

I began to walk her through forgiveness by having her repeat after me, "I forgive you for violating me. I forgive you for stealing my innocence. I forgive you for taking what was not yours to take, and for being selfish."

I spent awhile walking her through each trespass, and then we prayed a prayer of blessing over both of them. She left the prayer line that night completely revived, having the weight of her emotions about her past lifted off of her. For the first time in years, she was free!

The Freedom Keys to Forgiveness

Let me reiterate the essential keys to freedom when helping yourself or someone else get free from the bondage of pain:

- Connect with the trauma instead of running from it.
- Verbalize (privately or with a trusted counselor) how the violator caused you to feel.

- Ask the Holy Spirit how He views the violator and experience His compassion for the person; then pray a
  prayer of forgiveness for the violator.

These are the fundamental components of experiencing the
Father heart of God in the midst of a painful situation.

Unforgiveness is a relentless taskmaster that guards the
dungeon of past offenses. Forgiveness is a choice, but it's not an
option for anyone who wants to live a joy-filled life. It's important to remember that forgiveness is an act of the will, not an
act of the emotions. Therefore, you cannot measure the depth
of your forgiveness by your feelings. When Jesus forgave us for
all of our sins, He gave us the power to forgive everybody who's
wronged us. We know when we have truly forgiven, because we
no longer want the one who has wronged us to be punished.

Sometimes forgiveness is like a seed planted in the good
soil of your heart. As you water the seed of forgiveness by reminding yourself over and over again that you choose to release
from punishment the person or persons who have harmed you,
the pain in your soul begins to dissipate. Once you have made
the right choices, your wounds stop festering and your heart
heals. Although this process may take time, you can be assured
that you will fully heal.

CHAPTER 9

True Love

I climbed into bed exhausted from the workings of a demanding day and quickly fell into a deep sleep and began to dream. In what felt like only moments, I found myself trapped in a room made of glass. It wasn't long before I realized this place was like no other place I had ever been before. In a panic, I searched for an exit, but there was none.

My anxiety increased as I began beating my fists against the walls of glass, trying to bust through. Then my terror turned to wonder as I realized the walls were solid, yet fluid and alive. As I pushed against them, I began to feel a strong current of emotion flowing through the walls, like what you'd feel if you were standing in a river. As I leaned into the wall, the weight of love for the whole world fell so heavily upon me that I dropped to my knees.

It was in this moment that I realized I was caught up in eternity, held there by an unknown force. Overwhelmed by this intense feeling of love for the world, I began to peer deeper into the wall. The further I looked inside, the more I could see what looked like billions of movies of all kinds. I began to realize what was going on. These were not movies at all, but the lives of people in motion right before my eyes. With my heart pounding, I began to ask questions out loud, not necessarily expecting an answer.

"How did I get here?" I shouted.

Instantly, as if the question had been anticipated, a voice answered back, "I brought you here." His words burned deep into my heart. I had never felt that kind of compassion before.

As He spoke, His presence began to encompass me like a thick fog. I could feel holiness radiating through every cell of my body. For the first time in my life, I felt pure love, and the weight of the world lifted off of me. Lying face down, I could sense His excitement building as I was connecting to His heart and His thoughts became my thoughts. "I want to show you why I brought you here," He said.

I COULD FEEL HOLINESS RADIATING THROUGH
EVERY CELL OF MY BODY. FOR THE FIRST TIME
IN MY LIFE, I FELT PURE LOVE, AND THE
WEIGHT OF THE WORLD LIFTED OFF OF ME.

A movie of my life began to run in reverse, right in front of my eyes . . . rewinding past my birth, past my conception and into eternity. As the movie unfolded, I could see myself standing with God in a timeless place . . . before the earth was created. He pointed to me and said, "I knew you here!" Then He fast-forwarded the movie to conception in my mother's womb. I watched as God carefully formed me. A set of blueprints with my name on it appeared, and I watched as God built one-of-a-kind attributes into me. Talents, abilities, personality and looks were meticulously fashioned in my mother's womb, according to His perfect plan.

Next, He reached into my heart and planted a deep purpose for being me . . . something that no one else could ever fulfill, a call that only I could accomplish. As I watched Him form me in silence, I realized that each of my attributes were actually a piece of His likeness. Therefore, people could experience a part of God by observing my life.

When the movie ended, He picked me up, sat me in His lap and held me so tight. He said, "You're my favorite . . . you've always been my favorite!" His words ran like liquid love through my body, bringing healing to every broken place in me and setting me free.

In His Image

Thousands of years ago, God spoke to the prophet Jeremiah and said, "Before I formed you in the womb I knew you" (Jeremiah 1:5). In Genesis 1:26, God said, "Let us make man in our image, in our likeness." Think about that for a second . . . the most amazing, beautiful Master Craftsman created us in His own image! This is an incredible statement about how we were made!

The second thing that's important to know about these verses is that God had our history planned before the beginning of time! If He knew that we were going to be born, then He must have a plan and a purpose for our life, because God doesn't make mistakes.

The apostle Paul wrote, "In him we were also chosen, having been predestined according to the plan of him who works out everything in conformity with the purpose of his will" (Ephesians 1:11). We were created by divine design! God is not sitting up in heaven wondering what He's going to do with all these people who are being born.

One of the greatest violations of our relationship with Christ is to misunderstand who we are and how we were made. When we devalue ourselves, we are diminishing the Creator, because we were made in His image. Not only that, but when we received Christ, He did a brain transplant on us. He took out our brain and gave us His, which is why the Bible says, "We have the mind of Christ" (1 Corinthians 2:16).

The Truth About Love

Many Christians have been taught exactly the opposite. If you remember back to the story of Jody, her greatest problem was that she didn't love herself and she couldn't forgive herself. Usually the hardest person in the world to forgive is ourselves! These two things added together equal a broken-down, arthritic Bride, begging for her Husband to come back and save her, instead of a victorious Bride who is bringing heaven to earth!

Most of the world's problems are rooted in self-hatred, because we will never let somebody love us more than we love ourselves. That is why Jesus said, "Love your neighbor as yourself" (Matthew 22:39). If we don't love ourselves when somebody has a deep love for us, the thought of that person rejecting us is incredibly painful. So without even knowing it, instead of risking a major rejection, we do things subconsciously to sabotage the relationship in order to protect ourselves.

Another scenario that often plays out when somebody loves us more than we love ourselves is that we become overly dependent (codependent) upon that person because we are afraid of him or her leaving us. Therefore, we live our entire life at the mercy of another, instead of being able to set boundaries and share our most intimate needs, which is true love. That is why Solomon wrote, "Under three things the earth quakes, under four it cannot bear up," with the third thing being "An unloved woman who is married" (Proverbs 30:21,23).

The standard with which we love ourselves is also the standard with which we will love others. Without a doubt, if you don't love yourself, the chances of your loving somebody else according to God's standard are going to be slim to none. You can't walk around hating who you are and out of the very same vessel extend life and hope to the people around you. It just doesn't work that way! Loving yourself according to God's standard is the only way that you will ever actually have truly happy and healthy relationships.

LOVING YOURSELF ACCORDING TO GOD'S STANDARD IS THE ONLY WAY THAT YOU WILL EVER ACTUALLY HAVE TRULY HAPPY AND HEALTHY RELATIONSHIPS.

There are so many different opinions about love and what it is that it feels foolish to go any further without defining it.

Love is not a fleeting emotion that comes and goes with the wind. Nor is it a spark that was created in a combustible moment of euphoria. Love is a choice! Love is sacrifice! Love is boundaries; and yet, love is unconditional. The most beautiful living model of love that we've ever had on earth is Jesus. He was and is the embodiment of true love. He took care of Himself and His own needs, yet He was powerful, and He gave. He brought the best of Himself to every situation and used it to build the best in others. And finally, He yielded Himself to the whip and to the cross to restore our relationship with the Father. Jesus said, "Greater love has no one than this, that he lay down his life for his friends" (John 15:13). Jesus' ability to lay down His life and build others up rested in the fact that He first loved Himself! He knew where He came from and what the Father had commissioned Him to do; therefore, He knew how unique He was and what He had to give.

Who Do You Say You Are?

It's not enough just to know what the Scriptures say about you, because your identity doesn't lie in your head, it is embedded in your heart. Jesus said, "The good man brings good things out of the good stored up in his heart, and the evil man brings evil things out of the evil stored up in his heart. For out of the over-flow of his heart his mouth speaks" (Luke 6:45). Who we are and what we believe to be true about ourselves is derived from multiple places.

If you are starting out behind the curve, and you're reading this book saying to yourself, *I don't think I love myself like I should,* you first need to go back and reread my dream about creation at the beginning of this chapter so that you can recall how God made you and how He sees you. Spend time every day going over these truths until they become yours.

TREAT EVERY THOUGHT THAT'S DANGEROUS
TO YOUR IDENTITY OR CONTRARY TO WHAT HE
SAYS ABOUT YOU AS A TRESPASSER.

Next, "Take captive every thought to make it obedient to Christ" (2 Corinthians 10:5). Treat every thought that's danger-ous to your identity or contrary to what He says about you as a trespasser. These thoughts are evil by nature and are only there to erode your identity. You have permission to tell any thought that does not line up with God's Word to leave your mind.

Now, let's check how you talk to yourself! Positive self-talk has to be such a huge part of the life of a believer in order for us to be healthy and whole. Take a look at what happened to you last week and ask yourself how many times you had thoughts in your head that were not from God. Bethel Church's senior pastor, Bill Johnson, says, "We can't allow ourselves to have a thought in our head that is not in His." How many times did you talk to yourself in a destructive way this week?

I often tell people who are struggling with their identity, "You have permission to catch yourself at red lights thinking about how awesome you are!" The religious spirit says, "You're going to drive people into pride!" But the truth is that when we keep in mind that we were born to be amazing because we were modeled after Jesus and created by God Himself, then pride is the last thing we need to worry about. Pride comes most often when we are trying to lift ourselves up because of our insecurity.

Counterfeit Loves

One of love's greatest tragedies is that it's been mistaken for passion. True love is rooted in sacrifice—the laying down and the giving of life. Passion is an emotion that is felt most often in the pursuit and exploration of another. We shouldn't exchange passion for love. Nor should the pursuit of passion ever come before the foundation of love. When relationships are based on passion, emotion determines the depth of the connection, and before you know it, you're hearing statements from married couples like, "We just fell out of love." Give me a break! You can't fall out of love any more than you can fall into love!

Love is a choice. When couples make the choice to stop sacrificing and laying down their lives for each other, love goes dormant and the relationship begins to die. Passion is a healthy part of intimate relationships when love is at the core of the covenant. But if a couple uses passion as the glue to bond them together, the relationship will just be a flash fire instead of an eternal flame.

Love's promise is this: You will feel. A heart encased in steel feels nothing. After being deeply wounded by love and its many façades, I knew deep inside that in order to love again, I would have to risk again. But with so many hurtful brands of love in this world, I was tempted to throw away the key to the protective cage that surrounded my heart. If I was going to be able to hold the gates of my heart open, I would have to be watchful for love's many counterfeits.

Selfish Love

The first counterfeit is selfish love. This kind gives only for the purpose of getting back. It is usually short-lived, leaving behind flash fires and burned bridges. Selfish love is neatly packed in sweet talk and smooth moves, wooing its victim to vulnerability before dealing the fatal blow. The telltale sign of selfish love lies in its inability to sacrifice and serve another. When you find yourself in a situation with someone who is unwilling to meet anyone else's needs besides their own, feel free to tuck your tail and run!

> SELFISH LOVE IS NEATLY PACKED IN
> SWEET TALK AND SMOOTH MOVES, WOOING
> ITS VICTIM TO VULNERABILITY BEFORE
> DEALING THE FATAL BLOW.

No-needs Love

Another counterfeit is selfless love. Selfless love gives to anyone who demands it, with the hope of one day being able to fill the bottomless pit that is in his or her own soul. People like this have their identity wrapped up in the fact that they are the blood that keeps the leeches alive. Powerless people who pretend to have no needs usually offer this kind of love. But without the sharing of needs, love is never whole. In these kinds of relationships, there is only one powerful person, and it's not them. The underlying fear is that if they have needs and share them, they'll be left all alone.

Drunken Love

The third counterfeit of love is drunken love (also known as blind love). Drunken love is fueled purely by an intoxicated state of emotions, usually brought on by desperation and fear. This dangerous love pushes past all boundaries, failing to yield at warning signs, in pursuit of a fix. Drunken love is sure to leave you in a pile of sober regret with little or nothing gained. You can usually tell when you're in this situation because the community around you is screaming, "DANGER!" But the drunken lover justifies his or her intoxication with clichés like "Nobody understands me." Any time you're using this justification to stay in a relationship, you're in deep water!

My Life Now

When my marriage crashed, I learned a lot about myself. In the vulnerability of desiring to truly love others, I am continually urged to grow. Every relationship stretches me, and with each mistake or hurt, I have to make a choice to learn instead of run. Love is risky business, and there are no guarantees when it comes to trusting another person. My questions abound as the soil of my heart is continually turned over by the plow of relational process. I must understand how to love while using discernment regarding love's true nature. Love without a standard is not love at all. It is just brokenness trying to find a home.

There are many faces that mask themselves as true love; but when I have experienced their fruit, I have found they lack the attributes of all that love encompasses. Those who partake in these false loves think they have tasted the real thing but are left hurting. In order to find true love, I had to know its attributes. In 1 Corinthians 13:4-7, Paul beautifully describes true love's characteristics:

> Love is patient, love is kind. It does not envy, it does not boast, it is not proud. It is not rude, it is not self-seeking, it is not easily angered, it keeps no record of wrongs. Love does not delight in evil but rejoices with the truth. It always protects, always trusts, always hopes, always perseveres.

Love is freedom. Love is wholeness. Love is honoring. As I traversed down love's path again, I was reminded of this truth that I am the only one who has the power to decide what type of relationship I will be involved in. I control my standard.

Love is not love unless it costs me something. Love is not love unless it seeks only the highest good of the other person. Love is not love unless it leads to freedom.

LOVE IS NOT LOVE UNLESS IT SEEKS ONLY THE HIGHEST GOOD OF THE OTHER PERSON. LOVE IS NOT LOVE UNLESS IT LEADS TO FREEDOM.

Having been so wounded in a relationship and now having come out on the other side, I can see and appreciate love's amazing attributes. I realize now that God loves me unconditionally. After going through what felt like the end of my life, I recognize that it was not my choices that nearly killed me, but the choices of another. Regardless of her shortcomings and abuse of our relationship, I never lost my love for her or my hope for her to be whole. If I can go through that and love her in spite of all that's happened, how much more does God love me? After all, I am the person who put Him on the cross and broke Him with the whip.

CHAPTER 10

Red Flags

So many factors play into being an emotionally healthy person and living whole in relationship with others. *Peace* is one of those factors that you just can't leave home without.

Many times in my life, I have found myself in these epic battles, fighting for the possession of my own peace. These wars were not announced by the sound of a trumpet to warn of the presence of an opposing enemy, nor were there soldiers standing on a battlefield in plain sight, holding shields and spears. The battlefield was in my mind, and the opponents were the deceptive lies that had crept in undetected.

Since you are among the living, I'm sure you have experienced what I'm talking about. These opponents that we fight manifest themselves in the form of insecurity, anger, loneliness, rejection, self-pity, frustration, and so on. And though these feelings are not evil, if left unattended, they will become as destructive as the devil himself.

One of the most important things to know about these feelings is that they need immediate attention because they have so much influence over us. I refer to these feelings as "red flags." Every red flag, whether it is loneliness or insecurity or anything else, leaves you extremely vulnerable to the violation of yourself or another. It's important to know that at the end or beginning of a relationship, you will be most susceptible to these red flags.

About three months ago, I woke up at 7:00 A.M. to find that my brain had already been up and processing for quite some time. As I lay in bed, thoughts of insecurity rolled through my mind one by one, making themselves known to me. For a second, I thought about just pushing them aside and going back to sleep, hoping they would somehow just disappear. But the longer I lay there, the more I began to realize that these saboteurs were not going to leave peacefully. Insecurity slowly began to take over my entire soul to the point that it became all I could think about. Realizing this wasn't my normal state of mind, I had to make a decision: try to ignore it, or battle it out.

I decided that leaving the house with a starving heart and no peace was probably a really bad idea! And since I had the day off, I decided to spend the better part of three hours lying in my bed, battling it out, knowing that the consequences of walking around feeling insecure are costly. Here's why.

My job is to help oversee 800 School of Ministry students and 10 pastors, plus pastor 65 students of my own. Most of my duties as a pastor and as an overseer of the school land me in an office, counseling young students through their issues. If I walk into a room with a hurting student and I am feeling needy and insecure myself . . . I'm taking a very high risk of spilling my insecurity onto the person sitting across from me and infecting them with something they didn't walk in with.

Even if I don't necessarily negatively affect their peace of mind, if I somehow feel better about myself or less insecure because of what they say about me, then I have become a slave to the praise of man, and I will always be at its mercy.

Small Flames Become Forest Fires!

Throughout this book, I've given you multiple examples of people who have damaged themselves or someone else. Each one of those violations did not originally start as an infringement; rather, it began as a small spark that was left unattended and eventually grew into a forest fire of damage to others.

A great example of this, although admittedly a harsh one, is the life of Ted Bundy. Bundy was one of the most feared, cold-blooded serial killers of our time. But he didn't start as a hardened soul looking for blood. He began as a young man who, at the age of 13, got addicted to pornography. His addiction to soft porn dramatically increased as the years went on. Soon he craved more explicit and violent scenes, which eventually led him deeper into his addiction until he finally became the Ted Bundy we all know about.

I realize his story is an off-the-charts example of what happens with something that starts small, but the truth is that if Ted Bundy had taken care of the need he had in his heart at the age of 13, when it was just a spark, the lives of many, including his own life, would have been forever changed. But because he failed to find out what he needed, and get help, the spark of perversion and need for significance grew into a rage that cost many people their lives.

BECAUSE TED BUNDY FAILED TO FIND OUT WHAT HE NEEDED, AND GET HELP, THE SPARK OF PERVERSION AND NEED FOR SIGNIFICANCE GREW INTO A RAGE THAT COST MANY PEOPLE THEIR LIVES.

Dating is a less dramatic example of how unhealthy people can create dysfunctional relationships. In a dating relationship, it's really common for insecurity to drive the relationship faster than it should go, causing both parties involved to get to a place of intimacy without having the foundation of trust. No one likes to feel insecure in a relationship, but the lie is, "If I would just get to the point in this relationship where he/she was fully committed, then my insecurity would be gone." Therefore, the intimacy pace picks up and boundaries get crossed. Two years down the road, you are married and you discover that the foundation of trust is missing, and you're left scrambling to find your legs in the relationship.

On the flipside, if you know that you are feeling insecure in a relationship, and you take the time to deal with that insecurity, then both of you are protected. Instead of fear as the driving force of your relationship, your motivation for going deeper is built upon trust.

I could literally give you a hundred examples of things that started small and worked their way into massive issues. But the most important thing I want you to learn in this portion of the book is that any need—whether it is insecurity, loneliness, frustration, self-hatred, anger, or the like—that goes unchecked will eventually grow into something massive. It may not be today or tomorrow, but it's much like a sliver under your skin. Left unattended, that sliver will begin to fester and grow an infection until it's so painful that you don't want anyone to touch it. But until you remove the sliver, the infection will continue to grow.

The Importance of Self-awareness

Every person has a set of needs that, if unmet, will eventually lead to some kind of pain. Many people are extremely detached from what they really think, feel and need. The problem with this is that we humans are designed to get our needs met, regardless of whether or not we are conscious of them. And without being cognizant of what we really need, the chances of getting our needs met in a healthy way lessen dramatically the more unaware we are of them.

The process of becoming conscious of what you think, feel and need is called becoming "self-aware." Becoming self-aware is one of the greatest defenses we have. Without this ability, we walk through a battlefield without armor and with a large bull's-eye drawn on our chest. It's only a matter of time before we get shot through the heart by a poor decision we didn't even see coming.

WITHOUT SELF-AWARENESS, WE WALK THROUGH A BATTLEFIELD WITHOUT ARMOR AND WITH A LARGE BULL'S-EYE DRAWN ON OUR CHEST.

The process of becoming self-aware is not rocket science, but it is a practice that requires daily attendance and attention. There are several ways to actually become good at the skill of knowing what's going on in your heart. The first step is to recognize that you have needs that will require some kind of action. One of the best ways to help you find out what you need is to pay attention to how you feel. For example, if you're feeling angry, somewhere inside of you is a need trying to get met. Anger, for example, can stem from feeling powerless and out of control; so if you're feeling angry, just stop for a second and go back to the place that triggered the feeling.

There are many reasons why a person could feel angry, but if you go back to where your anger began, you will find the answer to why you feel that way. You may not be able to solve the main problem that brought about the anger, but you can decide what you're going to do with your anger. Paul said, "In your anger do not sin" (Ephesians 4:26), which means that there is no shame in feeling frustration, insecurity or anger. It's what we do with our feelings that matters in life.

Explore the Benefit of Journaling

Another really great way to find out what you need is to spend time alone, writing in a journal without editing your thoughts. I often begin journaling not even knowing how I'm feeling or why I'm feeling a certain way; but by the time I am done writing out my thoughts and what happened in my day, I'm able to figure out where I'm at and why. In the same way, sitting down with a really close friend and talking through your thoughts and emotions can be an excellent way to figure out what you need and what is going on inside of you.

Take a Personality Test

There are two other factors that play heavily into the red flags of your life. The first one is your personality traits. All of us have a personality type with its own set of strengths and weaknesses. By learning what personality traits you possess, you can discover what fears you are prone to and what you tend to need to feel healthy and secure. Understanding your fears and needs will allow you to pay closer attention to those areas of your life.

When you develop a culture around you that takes into account your natural tendencies (for example, do you get more energy working in the spotlight or working behind the scenes?), you tend to live a more healthy and happy life. One of the easiest ways to discover your strengths and weaknesses is to take a test like the DISC test or a Myers-Briggs Type Indicator. These tests are designed to help you find out what personality type you are, which will aid you in developing a healthy environment internally and externally.

Identify Your Greatest Unmet Need

The second factor that will really help you become self-aware is to discover your greatest area of pain. For example, if your life has been riddled with rejection, then you know without a doubt that rejection waves a red flag for you. When you are feeling rejected and you aren't self-aware, you can easily slip back into an old pattern of isolation that takes you down.

In the midst of the darkest days of Heather's betrayal, I discovered that my greatest red flags were insecurity and loneliness. In one day, I went from being a husband married to a beautiful wife, to waking up in my bed alone. Some mornings, waking up alone felt like a cruel game that love had played on me. With my wandering mind, I could picture him and her lying together in each other's arms in the comfort of their own home. And although that may have been real, the truth is that before I even got out of bed on a morning like that, I had some pretty major emotional needs that had to be taken care of in order for me to be okay.

Insecurity and loneliness for a guy in my shoes is par for the course; it's even expected. It would've been the epitome of foolishness for me to be unaware of the presence of these emotions. But I quickly learned that loneliness and insecurity were no friends of mine, and anytime they showed their face on my property, I drove them out with a vengeance.

How to Deal with Each Red Flag

We don't get to decide who comes to our door, but we do have a choice whether or not we let them in. We have to appoint ourselves as the keeper of our lives and the protector of our hearts. We choose our moods, actions and belief systems; therefore, we are powerful enough to change them!

As a leader of a men's sexual purity group, I have discovered that most people's setbacks are the fruit of not recognizing the small spark of hurt until it becomes a forest fire. For many, the cycle of rage out of control has been a part of their entire life up to this point because of their inability to figure out what they need and get it met in a healthy way. You have to have a plan for each red flag you deal with in life.

When I was in the dark valley of my own circumstances, I would wake up each morning and ask myself out loud, "How am I doing? What do I need? Am I hurting . . . or is my heart doing good?" I found out that just taking a little bit of time to know myself every morning made me feel valuable; and usually, if something was off, even just a little bit, I could take care of it quickly because I kept short accounts with myself. Whenever I couldn't quickly drive away the afflicting feelings, I knew it was time for war. I had already made up my mind that leaving my house with any type of red flag waving from my soul was a really bad idea.

There are probably hundreds of ways to defeat feelings of insecurity, loneliness or hopelessness. But before you can overcome these enemies, you have to understand the root issues of your heart, as we talked about earlier in the book. There is a huge difference between *I'm feeling insecure because of something that just happened in the moment* and *I'm feeling insecure because I don't know that God is my Father.* These two issues are worlds apart and require different kinds of attention.

Ultimately, the way to get rid of red flags that are the offspring of someone else's actions is that we figure out what we need and we meet it accordingly. When I would wake up feeling incredibly insecure, I would spend hours lying in bed talking to God and journaling what He said about me and how He sees me. If that didn't take care of the issue completely, then I would call my dad and get some help.

Insecurity, fear, hopelessness, depression and self-hatred are all rooted in lies. The Bible tells us that when Timothy was having a struggle with fear, his spiritual father, Paul, wrote these words to him: "God has not given us a spirit of fear, but of power and of love and of a sound mind" (2 Timothy 1:7, *NKJV*). The greatest trump card we have in our pocket at all times is the power of the Holy Spirit and the Word of God. His power transforms our fears into peace, and His Word uproots the lies that get planted in our hearts.

THE GREATEST TRUMP CARD WE HAVE IS THE POWER OF THE HOLY SPIRIT AND THE WORD OF GOD. HIS POWER TRANSFORMS OUR FEARS INTO PEACE, AND HIS WORD UPROOTS THE LIES THAT GET PLANTED IN OUR HEARTS.

You Can Only Control Yourself

The book of Galatians teaches us that self-control is a fruit of the Holy Spirit's involvement in our lives (see Galatians 5:23). In this life there are a lot of things we need and want that won't get taken care of, because we have no control over the world around us. In fact, it is only by the Holy Spirit's power that we have control over ourselves! If we have any other belief system besides the one that says, "I'm only in control of myself," we are living in deception. The only person on the entire planet that you can control in a healthy way is yourself. You can share your feelings and your needs with other people around you, but it is their choice whether or not they take care of those needs. With this in mind, you have to learn how to be a powerful person regardless of what anyone else in your world does.

People with a victim mentality see through a lens that shows them this view: "The world is against me. Everyone else gets what I should have. I'm always the one who is left out." You will know right away if you have a victim mentality because these thoughts go through your mind on a regular basis. Victims feel like their circumstances are everyone else's fault. If people would just do things differently or treat them another way, life would be good. The truth is that when you embrace this mentality, you are the one with the problem! The good news is that if you are the problem, you can fix yourself (but not anyone else) with the help of God!

You Can Think Yourself to Freedom

Paul wrote to the believers in Rome, "Do not be conformed to this world, but be transformed by the renewing of your mind" (Romans 12:2, *NKJV*). These Roman believers were former polytheists (they worshiped many gods); therefore, conforming to the thought patterns of their world would have meant that they were embracing Greek mythology. Paul taught them that they needed to proactively change the way they thought. Sometimes we all need a good brainwashing with the Word of God (see Ephesians 5:26)!

It is scientifically proven that our habits and thought patterns actually cut neurotransmitter grooves, or paths, in our brain. Our core belief system builds freeways that facilitate our thoughts along these pathways. Think about it like a path that's been cut through a dense forest. This path or pattern of thinking is what we have been driving on our entire life. When we make a conscious decision to change the way we think, all we have really done is put a No Trespassing sign on that path. Here's where the change process begins: We have to cut a new thought path into our brains that leads to wholeness. Just like sawing through a thick forest, cutting a fresh path is hard work! If we are not careful, we will become blind to the No Trespassing signs placed at the freeway entrances of our old patterns of thinking and wind up traveling back down that same dysfunctional and destructive road again, because it's so familiar and much easier.

When you are in a lot of pain, you are highly motivated to change. At first, you will do almost anything you are asked to do in order to rid yourself of your current status. But as time goes on and the pain lessens, the motivation to become well typically fades with the pain.

WHEN YOU ARE IN A LOT OF PAIN, AT FIRST YOU WILL DO ALMOST ANYTHING YOU ARE ASKED TO DO IN ORDER TO RID YOURSELF OF YOUR CURRENT STATUS. AS THE PAIN LESSENS, THE MOTIVATION TO BECOME WELL TYPICALLY FADES WITH THE PAIN.

One of the antidotes to breaking this pattern is to begin to set attainable goals. These goals will help motivate you long after your pain is gone. Wisdom says that you should look at your life from the end and work backward. You shouldn't be afraid to take a moment, sit down at the edge of your grave and think about your life. What do you want to be known as? What do you want God to say about you? What is going to be most important to you when you are lying on your deathbed? The answers to these questions should be the motivators of your life.

Pain is a very poor motivator and an even worse counselor. You can no more guide your life with pain than you can navigate a raging sea with a broken compass. It is vision for the future that is your life's compass. By following vision, you will continue to cut through the forest of your mind to create a pathway to freedom long after the pain is gone. A life lived in this fashion is a life that will be remembered for good!

CHAPTER II

Into Me You See

In early 2010, a young man came to me for help. This particular guy had grown up in our church, so I had known him for some time. John came into my office that day looking somber, like someone had drained the hope right out of him. It only took a few words from him to see why. He began to share with me the story of his recent affair, recalling to me the shame of losing his wife and the torment of the last few months.

As John recounted his story, the thought kept running through my mind: *Why would John cheat on his wife to whom he's only been married for a year?* As I questioned him, things began to come clear. On the outside, John was a fine gentleman who had been in church for most of his life. But on the inside, John was a dungeon full of tormenting dragons. His early childhood memories were riddled with searing pain. His dad used to tie him and his brothers to trees and beat them with rubber hoses to teach them a lesson. John's dad was a cold, unaffectionate man who taught his sons that true love came in the form of punishment. There was nothing John could ever do that was good enough for his dad; nor did John ever hear the words "I love you" from his father.

Early in his teenage years, John found the Lord while attending his church youth group. However, instead of this easing the pain, in some ways it was magnified. John was 12 years old, dying for affection on the inside, and among a group of kids who had what he so desperately needed. But it wasn't too long before John realized that if these kids found out that he was a dungeon on the inside, they would do what his father did—reject him. Unwilling to risk rejection, John learned the fine craft of hiding what was going on inside. He had numerous faces he showed to people, but none of them were real. They were all façades of who he'd really like to be, creations of his own imagination.

> UNWILLING TO RISK REJECTION, JOHN LEARNED THE CRAFT OF HIDING WHAT WAS GOING ON INSIDE. HE HAD NUMEROUS FACES HE SHOWED TO PEOPLE, BUT NONE OF THEM WERE REAL.

Time passed, and the pain continued to grow, fueled by the realization that people didn't love him; they loved a façade. John was unable to make the pain go away on his own. He began to self-medicate with pornography, hoping to somehow fill that place of intimacy that had never been filled before. But the pain was like a festering wound; the dungeon had grown darker, and the dragons had sunk their accusations deep into his heart. He knew himself only as a violator, of himself and of women.

John continued down this road through his teen years until he finally met his wife around the age of 20. At first, everything seemed great. She was exactly what he'd always wanted. He had spent his entire life trying to find someone who would really love him, and who he could love. How could this possibly go wrong? John wasn't married a year before the dragons began to remind him that his wife didn't really know him, because he had many faces, and all of them were frauds. The fear of ever being found out and rejected was compounded by the fact that the woman he had married was a gem. He thought, *If she ever finds out who I really am, she will never love me.*

The pressure continued to build inside of him as the days went on, and the dragons whispered their deceit into his ears. All the while he continued to go further inside of himself, trying to bury who he was. It was only a matter of time before a lack of true intimacy and his façades blew their relationship into a thousand pieces. Alone, and starving for affection, John went back to the only place he'd ever found comfort—to another woman just as broken and hidden as he was.

Repeating the Sins of the Father

John was repeating his father's sins. But what John didn't realize was that the sins of his father were not passed down through a hereditary disease of some kind; they were given to him by his agreement with his father's belief system. John never broke away from his father's core values. He clung so tightly to a dysfunctional mindset learned through his father's beatings and abused love that it finally cost him everything.

The truth is that John was a new creation in Christ. Old things had already passed away, and God had brought new things into his life (see 2 Corinthians 5:17). We often hear Christians ask, "If I'm a new creation, then why am I still dealing with the same old stuff?" The answer lies in our ability to fully submit our lives to Christ. Jesus said, "Come to me, all you who are weary and burdened, and I will give you rest" (Matthew 11:28). The essence of what Christ said is, "Come to me as you are: tired, weary and burdened, and I'll meet you there."

Most believers who are stuck in their sin have come to Christ the same way they came to the world: hiding behind their façade, playing church. Their intentions may be good but they don't understand that Christ is the way out. He's not looking for them to find a way out without Him! The truth is that we actually need Him in order to live victoriously! In other words, if we're going to get free, then we have to come to Christ just as we are. The book of Ephesians unearths an incredible revelation of the behavior of God's holy people:

> For you were once in darkness, but now you are light in the Lord. Live as children of light (for the fruit of the light consists in all goodness, righteousness and truth) and find out what pleases the Lord. Have nothing to do with the fruitless deeds of darkness, but rather expose them. For it is shameful even to mention what the disobedient do in secret. But everything exposed by the light becomes visible, for it is light that makes everything visible. This is why it is said: "Wake up, O sleeper, rise from the dead, and Christ will shine on you" (Ephesians 5:8-14).

This is a powerful passage written to Christians. Paul taught us here that we are not to hide in darkness; we are to bring everything into the light. When we come into the light, our souls are awakened from the dead and we *become* light! But what happens when we come to Christ, yet continue to hide pieces of ourselves in the shifting shadows of darkness? This was John's story. He came to Christ desperate, wanting to feel something he had never felt before, needing love and longing to be free. But he had only unlocked certain rooms of his heart to the Lord, keeping inside of him the dragons that haunted him because of his belief system.

The parts of his heart that he had opened up had become free and whole; but there was an entire world of darkness that the Lord did not have access to heal because John feared that his transparency would be punished. Therefore, John invited the ancient dragons of his old life into the beautiful palace of God's presence.

Fear of rejection feeds the monsters of our soul and shackles us to the serpent of old. If we don't come to Christ as we are (with our baggage, bondage and brokenness), then we never experience His unconditional love. This leaves us feeling like we have to perform for His acceptance. However, if we come to Christ as we are, and He loves us in the midst of our sin, then the shining light of the Lord brings wholeness to our entire life. Fear of rejection and the shame that once took us hostage will be broken off of us as we embrace His incredible grace and our new nature in Christ.

FEAR OF REJECTION FEEDS THE MONSTERS OF OUR SOUL AND SHACKLES US TO THE SERPENT OF OLD. IF WE DON'T COME TO CHRIST AS WE ARE (WITH OUR BAGGAGE, BONDAGE AND BROKENNESS), THEN WE NEVER EXPERIENCE HIS UNCONDITIONAL LOVE.

Original Intimacy

Like all of us, John was hungry for an intimate relationship with God, yet shame had imprisoned him in the Garden with the serpent, which is so reminiscent of our founding father and mother. We all know the story of Adam and Eve and the cunning serpent that introduced sin into the world. Let's take a journey back to the Garden, the place where it all began, and see if we can discover the real roots of intimacy.

The story begins with God creating man both male and female, and then commanding them to be fruitful and multiply and subdue the earth (see Genesis 1:26-28). These verses may sound a bit perplexing because some believe that in Genesis 1 God is talking about Adam (Adam is the Hebrew word for *man* or *humanity*) being both "male and female," yet Eve hasn't even come onto the scene yet. In fact, these verses in Genesis 1 give us a birds-eye view of how God created humanity "male and female," while Genesis 2 gives us the close-up view of how and why God created Adam, the first man, and then designed Eve to be the perfect counterpart for Adam.

I understand that there are many ways to view the creation story in Genesis 1–2. One idea is that God created Adam having both male and female parts (a strange thing to try to picture, I know). Another explanation is that God created both male and female Adams. It's interesting to note here that the Hebrew word for "female" is not the same as the Hebrew word for "woman." For example, it's proper to say that the gender of a dog is female, but you wouldn't say that a female dog is a woman. Another possibility is that the first man, Adam, was created with only male parts, and God only created the corresponding female parts when He designed and created the woman to be the perfect counterpart to Adam.

The most commonly held view of the creation story is that Genesis 1 is the overview of God creating the world, while Genesis 2 holds the details of how God brought forth man and woman into the world. The strange thing about this explanation is that it leaves Adam looking for a suitable helpmate among the animals. In other words, if God's original plan for Adam was to be fruitful and multiply and rule the world, then it makes no sense that Adam would be placed in a garden with no ability to reproduce. And certainly, he was not searching among the animals for something that he could reproduce with. God made it clear from the beginning of creation that every species of creature was only to reproduce "according to their kinds" (Genesis 1:24). For these reasons, it becomes clear in Genesis 2 that the Lord wanted Adam to discover that there was no suitable helpmate for him among the animals so that Adam would desire what God already had in mind for him—a counterpart after his own kind, with whom Adam would serve Him by being fruitful, multiplying and ruling as servant-leaders over the world.

Okay, by now you are probably asking yourself why we are having so much dialogue about the creation of man. How does the origin of man and woman give us any insight into the roots of intimacy? Well, that's a great question. The answer lies in the original design of man. Adam was created to need God. Without God, Adam was incomplete and lonely. Whenever God came into the Garden in the cool of the day, Adam was whole, happy and fulfilled. But when God was gone, Adam was incomplete. Adam needed a helper suitable for him (see Genesis 2:18).

The Hebrew word for "helper" is *ezer*. It is used 19 times in the Old Testament: three times for woman, and 16 times for God. In other words, God was not looking for somebody that Adam could reproduce with. He was looking for someone who could be intimate with Adam in the same way that God was intimate with him. God solved the dilemma by putting Adam to sleep and taking the woman out of the man. He literally broke Adam in half so that Adam would be incomplete without his woman. Adam's need for his woman to complete him was so powerful that he immediately prophesied that "a man will leave his mother and father and be united to his wife, and they will become one flesh" (Genesis 2:24).

Adam and Eve enjoyed a life of ease. They walked with the Lord in the cool of the morning, and I imagine at night they lay in the grass at twilight and enjoyed the stars above. But unfortunately, this life of peace and intimacy with God and each other didn't last long. They disobeyed God by obeying the devil. This led to them eating from the only fruit tree in the entire Garden that God had forbidden them to eat. To make a long story short, after sinning, for the first time, Adam and Eve both realized that they were naked, and they hid from the Lord, covering themselves with fig leaves. Shortly thereafter, they were removed from the garden and left to fend for themselves amongst the wild.

Why We Hide

I want to bring just a few things to light from this story. When sin is introduced into our lives, we begin to hide, like Adam and Eve. Once sin takes root it starts to damage the most important part of our life: *intimacy with God and with others*. The day that Adam and Eve fell was the first day they no longer felt accepted, naked as they were. The level of intimacy with Christ was severely damaged by the sin that had crept in. And for the last 2,000-plus years, the greatest attack on mankind has been designed to isolate and choke out intimacy in our lives.

I hear people say all the time in Christian circles, "God is all we need." Now, on one level I understand what they're trying to say; but the truth is that we need more than God! That's exactly why He partnered Eve with Adam. Without the ability to let people into our life, we are anemic, starving for affection. As we talked about before, God is our source for love, identity, security, protection, provision and our future. However, the function that people play in our lives is the role of the helpmate.

People are your source for companionship, a sense of belonging, feeling known and understood, partnership, fun and many more things. People also do things like bring inspiration into our lives; they remind us of who we are, and they stand beside us in the toughest of times. We were never created to live on our own, or to only need God. He created us to live unified with Him and with other human beings.

Defining True Intimacy

Intimacy can be defined as "into me you see." It is the ability to open up and let the people around us know what we really think, feel and see. Intimacy is not just wearing our heart on our sleeve, but it's handing our heart to the people we love the most. It is in this most vulnerable state that we are able to receive love's fullness.

INTIMACY IS NOT JUST WEARING OUR HEART ON OUR SLEEVE, BUT IT'S HANDING OUR HEART TO THE PEOPLE WE LOVE THE MOST. IT IS IN THIS MOST VULNERABLE STATE THAT WE ARE ABLE TO RECEIVE LOVE'S FULLNESS.

Earlier in the chapter, I talked about coming to God as you are, so that you can receive from Him the love that He has for you. The same principle applies to people: if you show someone what's in your heart, regardless of what it is, and that person loves and accepts you, then you've experienced unconditional love, the kind of love that God has for you.

Without intimacy, we really have no way of getting our needs met. This was John's dilemma. He could never feel loved and accepted by the people around him because he had never been honest with them. Dishonesty imprisons us in walls of glass and isolates us from the affection we so desperately need.

Counterfeit Intimacy

I was teaching a class on discipleship a while back. During one of the Q&A sessions, a student asked me, "If you could give the world any one thing, what would it be?" After thinking for a while, I said, "If I could hand the world anything, I would give each person the ability to live a life of intimacy."

Our world is starving to be known and loved. That's why pornography and prostitution are two of the largest industries in the world. Pornography is a counterfeit form of intimacy. I have found that most of the people I've worked with who struggle with pornography have major intimacy issues. Pornography gives you a momentary feeling of being known and vulnerable without the risk of being rejected. This industry has continued to grow because of our lack of understanding of and our inability to reverse the damage that previous generations created.

OUR WORLD IS STARVING TO BE KNOWN AND LOVED. THAT'S WHY PORNOGRAPHY AND PROSTITUTION ARE TWO OF THE LARGEST INDUSTRIES IN THE WORLD. PORNOGRAPHY IS A COUNTERFEIT FORM OF INTIMACY.

In the sixties and seventies, the world rebelled against a society that had tried to get them to conform to the "rules." Young people were tired of tradition and religion; they wanted something real. The world shouted out with songs of reformation, singing, "All we need is love." Free love was the motto of the times. Kids all over the world were living the party lifestyle and exploiting their freedom. The confining rules of the forties and fifties had left the young generation starving for freedom and hungry for love and unconditional acceptance. However, the love and acceptance that humanity tried to create through the sixties and seventies only left people more broken and confused than when they started.

Giving the most visible part of ourselves to anyone who wants it only leaves us broken in the end.

Appropriate Levels of Intimacy

Although the baby boomers' needs were valid, the tactics of those times were ultimately damaging. What they failed to realize and protect was that there are actually different levels of intimacy; it shouldn't be dished out at the same level to everyone.

This is really the only way that intimacy remains valuable and we stay safe. The level of intimacy that we have with a person should always match the level of commitment. For instance, in a dating relationship, it's common for couples to kiss, make out or even have sex long before they've even made any kind of commitment to each other. You can imagine what happens if you've given yourself to somebody and then the next day they're done with you. The only thing you're left with is a pile of pain and a broken heart.

Because people have not understood how to set the boundaries of intimacy, it has become an incredibly dangerous thing to do. In relationships, whether it be with a guy friend or girlfriend, be sure that your level of commitment matches your level of intimacy.

What Supports Intimacy

Trust is the foundation of true intimacy. Trust is built through consistency, knowing that the other person has your best interests in mind. Trust is not built by the absence of mistakes, but rather on how well we clean up our messes. There is no one who is perfect in this world, so we make mistakes in our relationships. Yet, if our mistakes are dealt with in honor and integrity, it actually breeds greater trust in our relationships.

I once read a business book where the author had done surveys on this very topic. He polled customers from all over America, breaking them up into three categories: in the first category were people who had done business with a certain company and never had a problem with them. The second group of people were customers who had a problem with a company but the business had satisfactorily solved the issue. The third class of people were customers who had a problem with a certain company, but the dilemma went unresolved. Surprisingly, what the author discovered in his survey was that the most loyal customers were the people who had an issue with a company, but the business resolved the problem to their satisfaction.

If we learn how to clean up our messes and we make things right with people, we build loyal, trusting, intimate relationships.

Tactical Training for Intimacy

Fear of intimacy does not somehow vanish on its own. It's not like you wake up one day ready to share the depths of your heart with the people around you. But what I've discovered is that if you can learn good communication skills, you can counteract the fear you often feel in intimate relationships.

It's a lot like enlisting in the Army and the very next day being dropped into the heat of a battle. Any one of us would be horrified. The thought of even planning a tactical maneuver or getting out of the bunker would be terrifying. Yet, if we trained in military tactics for months, we would be ready for battle. Without experience in warfare, we would still be afraid, but the skills we received from training would help to override our fear and breed confidence in us.

IF YOU CAN LEARN GOOD COMMUNICATION SKILLS, YOU CAN COUNTERACT THE FEAR YOU OFTEN FEEL IN INTIMATE RELATIONSHIPS.

Developing good communication skills is a first step in overcoming the fear of intimacy. Learning how to articulate what's going on inside of you is especially important when things don't go as planned. We will talk more about communication in the next chapter. I recommend that you practice developing your skills with people who are safe. When you are in the beginning stages of overcoming hurt, it is not the time to go out and practice new skills among random people. You need to find someone or a few people, like a church home group, who can help you walk out this new lifestyle of transparency. What you are going to discover is that more people than you realize have lived through the pain of broken trust, betrayal and unhealthy relationships. Yet, as you learn how to live a victorious life, your breakthrough will become their breakthrough too!

CHAPTER 12

A *New Standard*

If I (Kris) am honest with myself, there is something inside of me (actually, inside of each of us) that says, "A person who messes up deserves to be punished!" One of the problems with this way of thinking is that we begin to define people by their mistakes instead of their created origin. A person who lies becomes a liar. A person who gets drunk is labeled an alcoholic. Whores, adulterers, pornographers and murderers are all alias names we give to people when we view them through their sin instead of through the lens of God's divine design.

The second that we connect people's sin with their identity, or label somebody by their worst action, we feel justified in punishing them. For example, in the church, I've often heard someone refer to a person as a "Jezebel" or a "Judas." The moment we name somebody after an enemy, we no longer want to reconcile with them. Instead, we are positioning ourselves to excommunicate them from our relational circle. The bonds of love are left at home, and the weapons of warfare are brought to the friendship banquet.

Creating a Culture of Reward

Identifying people by their failures creates a culture where rules replace relationship, and justice trumps love. It becomes more important to be right than to be together.

169

If you examine most of our social systems, you will find structures that are set up to punish people. We have become a rule-based society instead of a love-based one. "Redemption," "reconciliation" and "reward" are often hollow words in our culture. For example, when you see a police car following you, by nature you look down at your speedometer to make sure you are not speeding, because you understand that the officer is commissioned to find you doing something wrong, not something right.

> IF YOU EXAMINE MOST OF OUR SOCIAL
> SYSTEMS, YOU WILL FIND STRUCTURES
> THAT ARE SET UP TO PUNISH PEOPLE.
> WE HAVE BECOME A RULE-BASED SOCIETY
> INSTEAD OF A LOVE-BASED ONE.

Can you imagine a world where officials are charged with rewarding people for their accomplishments as their first priority? It might look something like this: You look in your rearview mirror and see a highway patrolman with his red light on behind you. You look down at your speedometer to assure yourself that you are driving well below the speed limit. An excitement begins to build in you as you make your way over to the shoulder of the freeway. The officer walks up to your driver's window, smiling. He says, "I've been following you for several miles and noticed how politely and safely you are driving. Here are two tickets to the Super Bowl. I hope you have a great time."

This example may sound crazy, but welcome to Kingdom thinking. When we received Christ, we were transferred out of the kingdom of darkness and into the kingdom of God. We left the culture of punishment behind and moved into the New World of reward. The Lord reiterated this truth over and over again in the Bible. In fact, the last chapter closes with Jesus saying, "Behold, I am coming quickly, and My reward is with Me, to render to every man according to what he has done" (Revelation 22:12, *NASB*).

What About Redemption?

The religious spirit wants to protect rules rather than relationships. The New Testament tells us that the Pharisees constantly scolded Jesus for breaking rules. When He would heal somebody on the Sabbath day, the Pharisees would get all pushed out of shape about it. Then Jesus would remind them, "The Sabbath was made for man, and not man for the Sabbath" (Mark 2:27, *NASB*).

Rules, laws and policies should always serve the redemptive purposes of God. Whenever societies require people to serve the rules above serving the people, crucifixion is always the outcome. Our American prison system, in many ways, has become an example of a culture of punishment, and not redemption. The goal of much of our justice system is to punish criminals rather than rehabilitate them.

Let me make it clear here that when people cannot control themselves internally, society is obligated to control them externally, in order that society can remain healthy and safe. But when we make it our job to punish people for their sins, we lose sight of society's primary role of redeeming and restoring people. If we believe that sinners need to be punished rather than redeemed, and that sin requires separation, we create a dysfunctional civilization. Of course, structures of punishment are always created in the absence of the awareness of our own need for God's redemption and forgiveness. It seems funny to me how people, in need of so much mercy, can be so judgmental.

Rebuilding Trust

One of the greatest challenges in building a redemptive society is the question of how we actually help people rebuild trust and restore relationships. We're all aware that without a supernatural intervention from God, change is often a difficult process that requires unknown amounts of time and patience. We certainly can't change somebody else, but we can create an environment that fosters the redemptive process for people who are in the midst of their metamorphosis.

A friend of mine is a great example of someone who brought sin into his houseful of kids through his 40-year porn addiction and then had an encounter with God that empowered him to change. As you can imagine, he encountered a lot of resistance from his family who desperately wanted him to change yet found it difficult to ever trust him again. Because sin cuts so deep, the first reaction that someone encounters on the path to restoration is usually based in fear. For so long, the family had been trying to keep his toxic behavior from completely destroying them. So each member of his family had built a system of defense against him, to the level that he caused each of them pain, in order to survive the environment that he created. Here's where it gets tricky: my friend is no longer living in sin and creating pain in his environment, but because he did it for so long and hurt his wife and children so deeply, the old way of seeing him is seared in their brains.

Understandably, over time, my friend's wife became the punisher, responsible for condemning his every sin, and his kids became distant. But he is no longer the man they still see him as! So, now what is he going to do? His wife is still playing the role of the punisher, and his kids are still distant, regardless of his change of heart and full repentance.

These are the circumstances in which most people decide that changing is too hard, and they fall back into the comfort of their old roles: my friend as the powerless one, numb to the effects of the punisher; and his wife dishing out to him the victim spirit by the shovelful. If he is ever going to change that dynamic, he will have to learn to love and forgive himself, and he will have to reset the standard for himself in the home.

God's View of Restoration

In the book of 2 Samuel, chapters 11–12, we find one of the most incredible displays of God's character in the midst of man's failure. We love to think about the heroic stories of King David, who killed a lion and a bear without a weapon, and slew a giant with just a slingshot and a pebble. David is the envy of every young man. Yet the man after God's own heart committed adultery and murdered his friend! If you're unfamiliar with this story, it goes something like this.

In a time when kings were supposed to go to war, David stayed home. That was his first big mistake. *The safest place in the world for us to be is in God's will.* We are more secure on a battlefield with God than in a fortified palace by ourselves. Nevertheless, David decided one night to take a leisurely stroll up on his roof patio where he looked down upon a woman taking a bath. David, in his boredom, sent messengers to summon the woman to come to him. That night romance filled the air as David had sex with one of his best friend's wives.

Months pass before Bathsheba brings David news that she is pregnant, and David's sin is about to be exposed. In a panic,

David summons her husband, Uriah, to come home from the battlefield immediately, knowing that if Uriah doesn't have sex with his wife, David's adulterous relationship with his wife will be discovered.

To make a long story short, Uriah came home from the battlefield, and in loyalty to his men, who were away from their families and sleeping on the hard ground at night, refused to sleep with his wife regardless of all of King David's efforts. Frustrated and scared, King David sends Uriah back to the battlefield, carrying his own death warrant. David had sent a letter with Uriah instructing Joab, his commander, to send Uriah to the front lines and then retreat from him so that he would be killed.

An honorable, mighty man fell that day on the battlefield of sin. When Bathsheba heard the news of her husband's death, she mourned for days. Afterwards, she married the king and moved to the palace. I'm sure David wished that none of this had happened. But the bad news continued and Bathsheba miscarried their first child. After mourning their child's death, David slept with Bathsheba again and she gave birth to the next king. They were instructed by God to name him Solomon.

This story demonstrates the redemptive nature of God. David's life is a picture of tragedy and triumph. Yet for me, the most beautiful part of the story is God's incredible ability to take a horrible situation and bring about His royal purposes. Solomon, one of the greatest kings in Israel's history, was born to parents who committed adultery and a father who had committed murder. But even more profound, King David is listed as the father (in the line of His direct forebears) of Jesus Christ (see Matthew 1:1; 9:27; 20:30; Mark 10:47; 12:35; Luke 6:3; 18:38; 2 Timothy 2:8; Revelation 22:16).

The life of King David reads like a soap opera, yet within its pages there is hope for everyone who has ever failed miserably and lived in regret. For those of us, who like David, have made destructive choices that have cost others, we need to remember that we can never fall so far that God can't find us, or fall so fast that God can't catch us, or fall so hard that God can't put us back together again.

> FOR THOSE OF US, WHO LIKE DAVID, HAVE MADE DESTRUCTIVE CHOICES THAT HAVE COST OTHERS, WE NEED TO REMEMBER THAT WE CAN NEVER FALL SO FAR THAT GOD CAN'T FIND US.

And for those of us who are the receiver of somebody else's poor choices, this story reveals God's heart toward destructive people. Long after the most merciful among us has thrown in the towel, the Lord is still there extending His hand of mercy and grace to people like us who don't deserve it.

That doesn't mean it's okay for people to live selfishly, destroying the lives of those around them. Sin itself has a way of carving up a person's soul. Much like the loss of Bathsheba's first child, unrepentant sin slowly but surely destroys the sinner. (Let me make it clear that a miscarriage or the loss of a loved one does not mean that it happened because you have sinned. We all know that bad things sometimes happen to really good people.)

Peter's Plight

Many of us don't relate to the life of a king like David. We are way too timid to identify with a giant-killer, too unassuming to connect with royalty, or we simply lack the passion that would leave a legacy that says we are a person "after God's heart." We are simple people who stumble through life, speaking out of turn and never seeming to get the answer right. Being impetuous, impatient and outspoken is our norm. For us, there is no palace, no royal processions or famous victories. The silver spoon was a wooden spoon in our youth. We were never the teacher's pet, the coach's choice or even the most improved player. We have never been the prom queen, won a beauty pageant or received a Grammy award.

We are everyday people. The world is filled with people like us. Our heroes are underdogs and rejects. We root for the disenfranchised and the broken.

> THE WORLD IS FILLED WITH PEOPLE
> LIKE US. OUR HEROES ARE UNDERDOGS
> AND REJECTS. WE ROOT FOR THE
> DISENFRANCHISED AND THE BROKEN.

Welcome to the life of Peter.

Through most of his early story he is revealed as a complete screw-up. He embodies the definition of socially awkward and spiritually dysfunctional. Yet Jesus loved Peter and patiently put up with him. He confronted his stupidity while speaking to his destiny.

Unlike David, Peter was no courageous warrior. When a little girl confronted Peter about being a disciple of Christ, just before the crucifixion, he denied even knowing Jesus. But that would be just one of three times that Peter would deny knowing Christ on that faithless night. Most of us would look at this as the ultimate sin. According to our standards, we would probably say that Peter had lost his faith and wasn't ever to be trusted again. But Jesus had other plans for Peter. Look at their dialogue:

> Jesus said to Simon Peter, "Simon son of John, do you truly love me more than these [more than other men love me]?"
>
> "Yes, Lord," he said, "you know that I love you."
>
> Jesus said, "Feed my lambs."
>
> Again Jesus said, "Simon son of John, do you truly love me?"
>
> He answered, "Yes, Lord, you know that I love you."
>
> Jesus said, "Take care of my sheep."
>
> The third time he said to him, "Simon son of John, do you love me?"
>
> Peter was hurt because Jesus asked the third time, "Do you love me?" He said, "Lord, you know all things; you know that I love you!"
>
> Jesus said, "Feed my sheep" (John 21:15-17).

What was Christ doing in this exchange? Remember, Peter denied Jesus three times. Jesus was giving Peter a chance to repent for each time he had denied Him! He was also saying to Peter, "Are you going to protect the things that are most important to me? Are you going to protect my heart?"

You would think that Christ would have said, "Peter, you have a rotten foundation. I can't build a great church with leaders like you." Or maybe He should have said something like, "You need a sabbatical, some time off to make sure that your commitment to me is pure." But instead, Jesus said, "I also say to you that you are Peter, and upon this rock I will build My church; and the gates of Hades will not overpower it" (Matthew

16:16, *NASB*). He reinforced to Peter that he was validated in Christ's eyes.

Paul's Plight

An even greater example of God's abounding grace would be the story of the apostle Paul, found in the book of Acts. Without going into much detail, before the apostle Paul was saved, he was a nightmare to the Christian world, slaughtering those who preached the good news of Jesus Christ. Paul had an encounter with the Lord while he was still a murderer. He got totally set free from his past and became one of the greatest apostles in history (see Acts 9). He wrote more than half of the New Testament, and his life is a monument to the redemptive power of Christ.

Perfect Love Casts Out Fear

Okay, by now you have probably figured out that God is not trying to punish you for your mistakes. In fact, His grace restores you back to the standard of glory that belongs to the Bride of Christ. But in order for there to be health in any relationship, it must be free from the fear of punishment. As long as you are afraid that you are going to be punished, love will be absent from your relationships. The Bible says that "there is no fear in love; but perfect love casts out fear, because fear involves punishment, and the one who fears is not perfected in love" (1 John 4:18, *NASB*)! If this is true, then it is also true that "perfect fear casts out love."

Let's go back to my original question about my friend who suffered from a porn addiction. What does a guy do who has brought so much heartache on himself and his family? There's really only one thing that is going to restore them to a healthy re-

178

lationship, and that is a new standard of love created by his true repentance. If your spouse was the punisher, and you have repented, it is no longer okay to let him or her keep punishing you!

IF YOUR SPOUSE WAS THE PUNISHER, AND YOU HAVE REPENTED, IT IS NO LONGER OKAY TO LET HIM OR HER KEEP PUNISHING YOU!

Here's an example from my own life. I remember one time when our kids were all teenagers. I got angry with Kathy in front of them and then treated her disrespectfully. The next day, I gathered the kids together in the front room and asked Kathy and each of the kids to forgive me. They all did and we went on with our day. About a week later, one of our boys came in the kitchen and started speaking sarcastically to Kathy. I walked in and told him that he didn't have permission to talk to his mother like that.

He said, "You were rude to Mom the other day yourself!"

I said, "Yes, but you forgave me. Forgiveness restores the standard. When you forgave me, you gave away your right to act that same way because your forgiveness restored me back to a place of honor. I repented. Repentance means to be restored to the pinnacle, the high place."

He told his mother that he was sorry, and she forgave him.

If we don't understand this principle, then the lowest point, the worst mistake or the stupidest thing we have ever done becomes our benchmark. For instance, if you were immoral as a teenager and later on in life you have teenagers yourself, you won't have confidence to correct them for their poor sexual choices, because you failed yourself in this area.

Failures that we have repented of are no longer the standard that we must bow to. When we asked God and those we hurt to forgive us, we were set back up to the high place that God assigned to us. Otherwise, the worst day of our life becomes the highest place we have the right to lead others. The truth is that forgiveness restores the standard of holiness in us and through us.

Matters of the Heart

The *King James Version* of Psalm 32:8 says, "I will instruct thee and teach thee in the way which thou shall go: I will guide thee with mine eye." This is a powerful statement from the most powerful Being. Have you ever thought about why you do the things you do? Why you serve the Lord and live a life according to certain standards? Is it because of the rhetoric that's been bored into you since your childhood? Or maybe the *Left Behind* books and movies really hit home and you don't want to be the only one left alone to fight all the crazy zombies?

If your reasons for serving the Lord and laying down your life for Him are anything besides love, you have already missed the mark. Jesus said, "Many will say to me on that day, 'Lord, Lord, did we not prophesy in your name, and in your name drive out demons and perform many miracles?' Then I will tell them plainly, 'I never knew you'" (Matthew 7:22-23). Why didn't Jesus know them? The reason is because while they were for God, they were not with God. Someone once said, "The main thing is to keep the main thing the main thing!"

What does this have to do with the restoration of relationships? Any time our intimate relationships major on doing all the right things instead of having the right heart, the outcome will be a massive disconnection. When God said that He would guide us with His eye, He means that we have to be close enough and intimate enough with Him to see what He sees. We also have to care about His heart enough to be moved by His compassion. In case you haven't already noticed, God is not going to force us to make good choices; He's not going to strongarm us into a right relationship with Him. He will *guide us* into an intimate connection with Him.

My friend who suffered with the porn addiction has to uphold the standard of Christ in his home, which means there's no punishment, and he also has to make his connection with his family his main focus. Just as Jesus dialogued with Peter, his family needs to know that he is going to protect their hearts! If their hearts do not affect his actions and attitudes, their relationship with him will continue to be damaged. It is the connection with his family that needs to be his guiding light and the motivation for their restoration.

I'm not only talking to people who have blown it; I am also speaking to the people who have been abused, like I was. The same principles apply to us. Once the person has repented and changed the way he or she thinks, you have to look for that person to make your connection together the main goal. If you don't allow the person to restore the standard of his or her life and see that person through God's eyes, then you will hold him/her to past mistakes through your judgments and ultimately bind both of you in a pit of destruction.

Resetting the Boundaries

Resetting the boundaries of your life means that you learn how to love yourself and others in a way that promotes health. I have already said it many times, but the only relationship you can do is one that doesn't include punishment.

Now, if you've made a huge mess, then you're going to spend a good amount of time repenting to people and cleaning up your mess. There'll be people who come to you a year later and say, "I'm still having a hard time because of what you've done." This is not the time to say back to them, "Well, I'm a changed person, so you just need to get over it!" This is the time to go back in your heart to the place of repentance you originally presented to them and do it all over again, if that's what they need!

I realize this can get really tricky, because often it's a spouse or a child that can't get over it and continually brings up the issue, refusing to change the way he or she sees you. Ultimately, he or she is not looking for restoration in the relationship, but for justice through punishment. In this case, you'll have to let this person know that his/her feelings and hurt are valid, but the only way to restore the relationship is to extend the same forgiveness to you that Jesus extended to both of you.

In resetting your boundaries, it's important that you don't send a big fat message that because Jesus forgave you, you're now free to act however you want. Rather, the message you want to send is that you know your actions and choices have caused a ton of damage. You have discovered the root issues of your heart that caused you to behave the way you did, and you're going to protect his or her heart by changing the way you think!

IN RESETTING YOUR BOUNDARIES, IT'S
IMPORTANT THAT YOU DON'T SEND A BIG FAT
MESSAGE THAT BECAUSE JESUS FORGAVE YOU,
YOU'RE NOW FREE TO ACT HOWEVER YOU WANT.

Like the Lone Ranger in the Wild West, old habits die hard. In restoring the boundaries of your life and the standard of your life, you'll have to be patient with the environment around you as people struggle to trust you again and see you differently.

Communication Is King!

I worked with my friend (the former porn addict) for months, helping him move out of the role of being the receptacle of his family's punishment, and teaching him how to communicate to them so that the way they were talking to him and treating him didn't feel punishing. I also taught him that his family had very real fears and needs that he must address. So, when his wife would begin to punish him, he had permission to stop her and say, "I'm feeling punished. Is there a way that you could re-phrase that statement, or is there something that you need from me without belittling me?"

Over and over again he would have to take a stand for him-self while making her heart a huge priority. Without setting new boundaries, he had no way of actually taking care of his family. His family didn't need a broken-down man; they needed a man with a standard, a man who cared about their hearts and who was going to teach them that they were valuable too.

At first, his newfound standard was met with fierce oppo-sition, because change is almost as scary as death. His wife had always been the punisher in the relationship, and he had never set a boundary that disallowed her abuse toward him. Over time and through lots of tears, he began to learn how to hear his wife's heart and also uphold the standard in their house by using statements like, "You sound really frustrated. Is there a way I can help you?" Or, "I'm trying to hear what you're say-ing, but when you throw judgment at me it makes me want to protect myself from you. Is there a way that you can say what you're feeling so that I don't have to feel defensive, and so that I can really hear you?"

Sometimes when his wife was feeling really frustrated and unable to change the way she was talking, he would have to try to stay in the conversation by saying something like, "Are you really trying to say . . . ?" whatever it was that he thought she was trying to communicate. Ultimately, he sent her a message that he really wanted to hear and validate her heart and lower her anxiety; but at the same time, he was unwilling to continue the dysfunctional cycle they had created in their life.

By persistently practicing good communication, you can push past your fear of being locked into your past, and give people a way to love you as you are now. Whether you know it or not, you are the one that teaches the people in your life how lovable you are. You show others how to treat you by the way you care for yourself, and by the way you allow others to treat you. All these things are your responsibility. No matter how wrong you have been in the past, Christ's forgiveness gives you permission to restore the standard in your life

Love Suffers Long

It was a cold February day when Jason entered my office looking as if he had seen a ghost. I (Kris) was already reeling from my oldest daughter's nervous breakdown that began two months earlier, so I was in no shape to hear more bad news. Jason plopped down on my couch, hanging his head.

"Dad, I think my marriage is over," he said, his eyes filling with tears.

"No way, son!" I protested. "God can fix anything."

"Dad . . . Dad, you don't understand, I think Heather is seeing someone else."

I could feel the blood rushing to my head as I fought off the tears that were forcing their way into my eyes. My mind swirled with thoughts as anxiety overcame my soul.

What's going to happen to my three little grandchildren if they divorce? I wondered. *How could a woman whom I loved like a daughter betray my son? Why would anyone who was loved by such an amazing man ever choose somebody else? I probably should've seen this coming,* I thought, because for several weeks, Jason had been telling me that their relationship felt like it was in shambles.

I knew they had been seeing a counselor for quite some time, but it seemed like the more he pursued her the further away she drifted. As he talked, I was rapidly becoming aware in my office that day that Jason had come to a point in his life where his heart was so broken and his hope was so deferred that he had nothing left to give. His marriage had crashed, and the only thing still remaining of their lives together was lying in pieces on the floor of my office.

I never thought it would actually come to this. Just two months earlier, Heather had stood on the stage with me in front of a couple thousand people, in Holland, and ministered powerfully to them. *How could she have been having an affair and still be used so mightily by God?* I wondered. Questions kept flooding my mind as I struggled to comfort my brokenhearted son.

I knelt down in front of him and threw my arms around him. There were no words . . . nothing I could say that could ease the pain. I just held him for a long time and reassured him that we would get through this together as a family.

I KNELT DOWN IN FRONT OF HIM AND
THREW MY ARMS AROUND HIM. THERE WERE
NO WORDS . . . NOTHING I COULD SAY
THAT COULD EASE THE PAIN.

The days ahead were unbelievably difficult for us. Although I'd had a terrible childhood—my father drowned when I was three years old, and I'd had two stepfathers who seriously abused me—I had never experienced pain like this before. Even now, words fail to convey the depths of my anguish as the facts were disclosed over the next several months.

At night, Kathy and I would crawl into bed exhausted, grieved and overwhelmed as we fought to find strength in God and the people around us. I reached deep down into my soul to find strength for my family, but my heart was bankrupt, incapable of encouraging anyone, much less myself. Most of the time we would lay awake deep into the night, tears flowing off of our pillows, puddling on the mattress beneath us. The pain seemed to increase with each passing day. It was like a nightmare we couldn't wake up from.

The day she moved out, Jason called and asked if he could bring the kids over to our house so that we could tell them together that their mommy and daddy were getting a divorce. "Of course," I responded. "Bring them over and we'll talk to them together." I wanted to comfort my grandchildren and help my son, but I was having flashbacks of my own conversations with my mother who was married three times. Twenty minutes later, they were at our door. My heart sank as I anticipated how they would take the news.

We all sat down in a circle next to the fireplace as Jason nervously broke the news to the children. Elijah, who was eight years old at the time, got up and ran to me and threw himself into my arms. Weeping uncontrollably, he shouted, "I don't want to live anymore . . . I don't want to live anymore!" Riley, who was six years old, buried her head in my shoulder and cried silently. Their tears soaked my shirt as I struggled to find words to console them. Evan was just four, so he was sad but didn't really understand the ramifications of the word "divorce." It was a night from hell . . . a time I will never forget as long as I live.

The black cloud of depression hovered over our family as days faded into weeks. It seemed like around every corner more pain and anguish awaited us. By the end of July, we learned that the guy with whom Heather was having an affair had left his own wife and child to move in with Heather, and shortly thereafter, we found out that she was pregnant with his child. Slowly the dagger of pain was driven deeper into our hearts as this nightmare continued to unfold.

It wasn't long before the cold weather of reality had begun to set in upon eight-year-old Elijah, leaving him angry and confused. Who could blame him? He was watching his mother live in a way that was diametrically opposed to everything he'd been taught. In his attempt to bring some sort of peace to his inner world, he confronted Heather and her boyfriend, letting them both know that he did not approve of their sleeping arrangements. But his words went unheeded, and he grew more distressed by the day.

Then one day, Elijah and I were driving down the road together. He was unusually quiet and seemed to be deeply troubled. After several minutes had passed, he turned and looked right into my eyes and said, "Papa . . . Papa, do you like my mama?" Tears welled up in his eyes as he stared deep into my soul.

I knew what he was really saying. He wasn't asking if I liked his mother; he was asking if *he* could love someone he so desperately disagreed with. Time stood still while I struggled to find the right answer for both of us. I knew the biblical response. The Scriptures about forgiveness marched across my mind like relentless soldiers on the battlefield of truth. But this wasn't a Bible class or some philosophical discussion; this was my grandson trying to fight his way out of the prison of bitterness so that he could comfort his siblings and embrace his mother.

Finally, with my lips quivering, I said, "Elijah, what kind of people would we be if we only loved people we agreed with? Of course I love your mother. I'm the only father she's ever had. I will always love her, no matter how badly she behaves."

Elijah blurted out, "I love her too, Papa! I love her too!"

It was as if someone had uncorked a bottle of champagne. His countenance suddenly brightened and his eyes glistened with effervescent liveliness once again. It was okay for him to love someone who had done so much damage to his life and to the people he cared most about. He was free from the bondage of having to change her in order to really love her. He had permission to show affection to the person who had betrayed him. He could live again, and he knew it.

MY GRANDSON WAS FREE FROM THE BONDAGE OF HAVING TO CHANGE HIS MOTHER IN ORDER TO REALLY LOVE HER. HE HAD PERMISSION TO SHOW AFFECTION TO THE PERSON WHO HAD BETRAYED HIM. HE COULD LIVE AGAIN.

My grandchildren attended the Christian school situated on our church campus. Heather would pick up the kids a couple times a week after school to exercise her visiting rights. I would often see her waiting in her car next to my office for the kids to get out of class. I pretended not to notice her sitting out there, and I made sure our eyes never met. Anger, betrayal, hatred and confusion filled my soul whenever I was confronted with her presence.

I had spent three debilitating months on the couch, overcome with depression and anxiety, because of her. She had destroyed my family and, honestly, I hated her for it. I didn't want to reconcile . . . I wanted her to pay for her sins . . . I wished for her demise every day. Of course, I was careful not to allow the seizing monster out of the basement of my soul. I said the right things, and I fed the angry monster in that rat-infested cellar of my heart at night. I didn't want anyone to know how toxic I was feeling.

Then it happened. I was standing in the parking lot, talking to someone, when she pulled up right in front of me. I am sure she didn't see me until it was too late. I looked over at the car that had rolled to a stop about a hundred feet from me. Our eyes met, and mixed emotions flooded my heart. Compassion and hatred were both warring against my soul. I stood frozen in the middle of the parking lot. I wanted to run away, but my legs would not submit to my emotions.

We stared at each other for what seemed like an eternity. Suddenly, the car door opened. Heather got out of the car and stood behind the driver's door. A few seconds passed, then she began running toward me. My heart was pounding out of my chest as she drew near. It was all happening too fast for me to gather my thoughts. Before I could move, she threw herself into my arms and buried her face against my chest. Her tears ran down my shirt as she wept uncontrollably. I felt like I was being torn in half. My head hated her, but my heart loved her. My head wanted to push her away and punish her, but my heart longed to embrace her and forgive her.

I FELT LIKE I WAS BEING TORN IN HALF.
MY HEAD HATED HER, BUT MY HEART LOVED
HER. MY HEAD WANTED TO PUSH HER AWAY
AND PUNISH HER, BUT MY HEART LONGED
TO EMBRACE HER AND FORGIVE HER.

"*Please . . . oh please forgive me!*" she wailed. "I have destroyed my family. I've ruined my life. I've messed up Jason's life, and I have broken the hearts of my children. I betrayed you and Mom. *Can you ever forgive me?*"

Just a month earlier, I had helped Elijah work through his bitterness with Heather by reminding him of the words of Jesus:

"If you love those who love you, what credit is that to you? Even 'sinners' love those who love them" (Luke 6:32). It seemed so much clearer when I was teaching Elijah how to love his mother. But now it was me who needed to forgive and to love.

I have never been the kind of person who could hide his feelings or pretend that everything was okay when it wasn't. I knew that whatever happened in the parking lot that day, I would have to live with for the rest of my life. I had preached many times about the grace of God that forgives our sins, restores our souls and heals our hearts, even when we don't deserve it. I thought about how it must have felt for Jesus to be betrayed by the very people He had fed, healed and delivered. How devastating it must have felt to look down from the cross and see people He so desperately loved, shouting, "Crucify him! Crucify him!" His words thundered in my head, "Father, forgive them, for they do not know what they are doing" (Luke 23:34).

I knew that once I said, "I forgive you, Heather," I would be giving up my right to punish her. That meant that she would be able to live happily ever after, even though she had wrecked my family, traumatized my grandchildren and betrayed my son. Not to mention the fact that when she got involved with another man, his wife was pregnant with their first child. She had helped to destroy his family as well. There would be another little child who didn't have his daddy because Heather lived selfishly and helped to lure him away.

Heather doesn't deserve to be forgiven; she deserves to be punished! I reasoned. But didn't I also deserve to be punished? Wasn't I forgiven while I was still a sinner?

The Scriptures became like soldiers, and my heart became a battlefield. What I preached so freely and eloquently from the pulpit was now warring against the battlements of my own soul. Honestly, I wasn't sure which side I wanted to win. Did I want forgiveness to win, and Heather to walk away with permission to live a happy life? Or did I want justice to prevail so that Heather would be locked away in a prison of her own choices for the rest of her days? The principle of forgiveness, which seemed so clear to me for years, was now clouded by my circumstances, emotions and my need for justice.

How would I feel if I saw Heather and her boyfriend laughing and playing together, while my son grieved over the loss of his wife? Would forgiving Heather be perceived as betraying my loyalty to my own son? If I showed Heather love, would she somehow get the idea that what she had done wasn't that bad? These questions were like grenades going off in my heart. The truth is, I had envisioned this day several times over the preceding months. My heart was filled with anxiety every time I pictured myself in this situation with Heather.

Finally, something powerful happened in me. I was suddenly overcome with compassion for Heather. It seemed to come out of nowhere. Just a minute earlier, I hated her, but now I hurt and grieved for her. I could feel her pain and I understood her sense of being completely overwhelmed by the mess that she had made.

I pictured her trying to claw her own way out of this deep, muddy pit of miry clay. Her fingers were bloody, her face was covered in dirt, and her hair was matted with sweat. She extended her hand for help. I stood there, bewildered by the sight of this beautiful woman so entrapped by her own brokenness. I reached my hand out and grasped hers. Blood and dirt covered me as I struggled to pull her out of the pit. But what touched me most was the look on her face when she saw me reach out to help her. Hope filled her eyes as if to say, *Thank you for dirtying your soul to rescue my life.*

The vision ended and I knew what I must do. I wrapped my arms around Heather and whispered in her ear, "I forgive you!

I forgive you, Heather. And I love you like I love my own daughters." Her weeping became more intense as I held her and spoke kindly to her.

"*I'm so sorry! I am so sorry!*" she kept repeating.

"It's going to be okay," I said to her, with faith filling my heart. "We're going to get through this together." I stroked her hair to comfort her.

We both knew in our hearts that their marriage was over. But life would go on, and Kathy and I would be there for her for the rest of our days.

We visited Heather many times over the next several months. Slowly but surely we were reconciling our relationship, and God was restoring our love for Heather.

On August 25, we received a phone call from Heather that she was in labor and was being rushed to the hospital. We were in Australia and couldn't get home until the next day.

When our plane landed, we went straight to the hospital. Baby Jackson was born the day before we got there. He was so cute with his tiny hands and feet. But baby Jackson unearthed another crisis in my own soul. I didn't understand the feelings I had for him at first. It really didn't make sense to me at all.

Then one day Elijah and I were together in the car again. Elijah, who typically is very talkative, was unusually quiet. It felt tense in the car. I tried to inspire some conversation between us, but he gave one-word answers to my questions, looking down as he spoke. It became increasingly evident that he was seriously troubled.

I wondered if he would open up and talk to me. We drove in silence for several minutes. Finally, Elijah looked up at me with tears in his eyes and said, "Papa, do you like Jackson?" Before I could answer, he asked me again (this time with more intensity), "Papa, do you like baby Jackson?"

I suddenly realized what he was asking me. Pondering the right answer gave me a revelation of my own struggle. What Elijah was really asking was, "Can I love the child who is the fruit of a relationship that destroyed my family?" I couldn't put words to the feelings I had toward baby Jackson until that day in the car. But when Elijah asked me if I liked Jackson, I found myself wanting to say, "*No!*"

It wasn't rational or an attitude that I had consciously cultivated. I knew in my mind that Jackson was as much a victim of the circumstances as any of us. He didn't ask to be born out of wedlock. It certainly wasn't his desire to be the fruit of an immoral relationship that destroyed two families. I actually admired Heather for not aborting this child and creating another tragedy.

Yet Elijah had uncovered a secret in both of our hearts. In some strange way we wanted to blame baby Jackson for the grief that we both felt. It was wrong, and I knew it. This misplaced attitude would be dealt with here and now.

ELIJAH HAD UNCOVERED A SECRET IN
BOTH OF OUR HEARTS. IN SOME STRANGE
WAY WE WANTED TO BLAME BABY JACKSON
FOR THE GRIEF THAT WE BOTH FELT.

I quickly gathered my composure and said, "Elijah, every child is a gift from God, no matter the circumstances of their birth. I love Jackson!"

"Papa, I love Jackson too!" he said, with tears now running down his face. "I love him too. He is so cute!" he said again for emphasis.

Jackson has become our eighth grandchild. A while back, our entire family, including Jason, Kathy and me, gathered in Heather's house for his first birthday. When Jason picked up Jackson and kissed and loved on him, I knew that we had tapped into a special place in the heart of God. I had this deep sense that God was bringing triumph out of tragedy and an amazing message out of this big mess: We were a living testimony that God comforts ALL those who mourn.

It has been more than three years since that terrible day when Jason stepped in to my office and told me that his marriage was over. There were many dark days when I questioned whether or not I could go on. I lay awake many nights with tormenting visions of our family's situation. I am embarrassed to admit that I often questioned God's ability to redeem our family, and I questioned the nature of His goodness. At times, I blamed myself for not being a better father and for encouraging Jason to marry Heather in the first place.

Those dark days have passed. I wish I could tell you that this story ends like a wonderful fairy tale, where Jason and Heather live happily ever after with their family. But sometimes real life is messier than that; yet God has a way of making beautiful palaces out of our painful pitfalls.

As of this writing, our entire family has a great relationship with Heather, with Jackson and even with her boyfriend. We're together pretty often and have cultivated a genuine love for one another.

All three kids are very well adjusted and doing great. By the time you read this book, Jason will have married a beautiful young woman named Lauren, whom we deeply love and admire. The children are excited to have Lauren in their lives and they have bonded very well with her. Heather has encouraged the children to have a great relationship with Lauren, which has really helped to keep the kids from being torn between two people they really love.

Love Suffers Long

In the mist of the darkest time of my life, I went to see a professional counselor who is a friend of mine. Of course, the first question he asked me was, "Why have you come to see me?" I told Jason and Heather's story and explained to him how discouraged and depressed I was over their situation.

He asked me again, "So, why have you come to see me?"

"I told you," I snapped back. "I'm discouraged and depressed."

He proceeded to ask me the same question again.

Finally, I asked in a very frustrated voice, "*What is your point?*"

"Well," he replied, "the Bible says that love suffers long. You are suffering because people you love are suffering. Jesus said that we are to mourn with those who mourn. You're in mourning because your family is suffering. You're responding the way that Jesus taught us to respond. When this is over, you will get to rejoice with those who rejoice. Until then, trust God with your family, and know that the season will end in time."

In an all-staff meeting a few months ago, Bill Johnson brought Jason (who is one of the pastors on our staff) up front. Jason announced his engagement to Lauren. Bill took the microphone and said, "We have mourned with those who mourned; now we get to rejoice with those who rejoice!"

About 200 of our staff were present that day. They stood to their feet and shouted, cheered and wept for joy. The Bible says, "Weeping may endure for a night, but joy comes in the morning" (Psalm 30:5, *NKJV*).

Keeping Hope Alive

Sometimes it's easy to think that God favors certain people, or that the situation we are in is somehow beyond God's ability to set us free (especially in the darkest of nights). I know these feelings all too well. But the truth is that there is no situation that is impossible for God.

One of my heroes is Abraham Lincoln. He was a father to our nation and a master of perseverance and hope. We know him as one of the most popular presidents in American history. Yet, it is Abraham Lincoln's list of troubles and failures that is the most impressive beacon of light and hope in the world. The list goes like this:

- 1818—His mother dies when he is nine years old.
- 1831—His business fails.
- 1832—He loses a bid for a minor post in the legislature.
- 1833—He goes into business again; competition from a larger company forces him to close down once again.
- 1833—His possessions are seized when he is unable to pay off his debts.
- 1835—His wife-to-be dies.
- 1843—He fails to receive his party's nomination for Congress.
- 1853—His son dies.
- 1854—He falls six votes short of securing an open seat in Senate.
- 1860—He is elected president of the United States of America (and again in 1864).

Talk about a guy who knew how to get up when he was knocked down! Wow!

Thousands of years ago, Solomon penned these words, "Where there is no vision, the people are unrestrained" (Proverbs

29:18, *NASB*). Abe Lincoln hung on to his vision in the midst of the darkest nights of his soul. There is so much truth held inside of these simple words. Vision keeps hope alive in us. Hopelessness is a serial killer. Without hope we have no faith; and without faith the world is a miserable place to live.

VISION KEEPS HOPE ALIVE IN US. HOPELESS-
NESS IS A SERIAL KILLER. WITHOUT HOPE WE
HAVE NO FAITH; AND WITHOUT FAITH THE
WORLD IS A MISERABLE PLACE TO LIVE.

God is the master of search and rescue. When everything looks bleak in our lives, we just need to look over our shoulder and we will find Him there. When Daniel was thrown into the lion's den and everything seemed dark and hopeless, God saved him. When Shadrach, Meshach and Abednego were tossed into the fiery furnace, Jesus set them free. When God found a man so bound with lies that he was murdering Christians, He encountered him on the road to Damascus and changed his name from Saul to Paul, transforming him into one of the greatest men of God who has ever graced this planet.

The stories go on and on of God's amazing ability to transform people. There was the demonized man at the Gadarenes; there was Lazarus, who had been dead three days; and there was Mary Magdalene the prostitute. There was Joseph who was sold into slavery but became a prince; and David who killed a giant with a rock.

There is no hand dealt to you that God can't win with. Whatever happens in your life, remember this: *Jesus is the master of making palaces out of pitfalls.* It's never too late for Him to redeem a situation. It doesn't matter how far you have fallen or how big a mess you've made out of your life, He is "able to do immeasurably more than all you ask or imagine" (Ephesians 3:20).

God specializes in the impossible; and despite how you're feeling . . . He is *for* you!

Acknowledgments

There are many things far greater than me alone; however, as a family, there are few things that we cannot overcome . . .

Through the rod, and equally by the affection of those I most adore, I have become me, and for that I am forever grateful. They say it takes a village to raise a child into a man, and I would add that it takes the courage of others to fulfill your dreams. Without the wisdom and courage of my father and mother, not only would this book still just be a dream of mine, but also life as I know it would cease to exist. You have been the lighthouse in the raging sea, shining your hope in the darkest of nights, reminding me that "this too shall pass," and giving me the guidance to set a steady course.

I believe that without the kindred affection of friends, a man is very one-sided. Just as it takes iron to sharpen iron, through the course of navigating relationships, friction and comfort are created, often showing the truth of a man to himself. Without the grinding wheel, the knife would never be sharp, and without one another, unconditional love with humanity would only be a theory. But through my closest relationships, my rough edges have become smooth and sharp. And because of a few men, I have been held accountable to being who God created me to be, knowing that I am always loved. Jerome E., Jeremy R., Mark P., Danny S., Jeff N., Keith A., Cameron R. and Marty P., and to the guys with whom I have shared my home, "thank you" feels like a hollow word compared to what you have given in sacrifice for me. Because of you men, I know that I will always have a safe place to process my emotions, or to be as wild as my heart desires in the safety of your presence. Thank you!

Lauren, there is not enough space on this page for all of the words I want to say to you. You are truly a lily among thorns; a gem among a sea of stones. Your encouragement and belief in me has meant the world to me. I could not have fashioned a greater woman to spend my life with—you are more than I ever imagined I would have. I can't wait to see what the power of two becoming one produces. I love you!

Jason

Kris Vallotton

Kris Vallotton is the author of several books and is a much-sought-after international conference speaker. Kris has a passion to see people's lives transformed and to be a catalyst to world transformation.

In 1998, Kris Vallotton co-founded the Bethel School of Supernatural Ministry in Redding, California, which has grown to more than 1,200 full-time students. Kris is the senior associate leader at Bethel Church and has been a part of Bill Johnson's apostolic team for more than 32 years.

Kris is also the founder and CEO of Moral Revolution, an organization dedicated to a worldwide sexual reformation.

Kris and his wife, Kathy, have been happily married for more than 35 years. They have four children and eight grandchildren.

For more information, please visit
www.kvministries.com

You can also find Kris Vallotton at
www.moralrevolution.com
www.facebook.com/kvministries
www.ibethel.org

Jason Vallotton

Jason Vallotton was born and raised in Weaverville, California, a small town known for its mountainous views and mellow pace of life. He got a quick start in life after getting married at the age of 18 to his high school sweetheart and fathering their three children by the age of 24 (Elijah, Rilie and Evan).

Jason's life has been riddled with challenges, from raising a young family and fighting fires through the hills of Northern California, to overcoming the heartbreak of his marriage dissolving in 2008. He has become a testimony to the redemptive power of perseverance and unconditional love.

Jason's love for people and his drive to see them completely whole has led him to Redding, California, where he helps to oversee a School of Ministry and a men's sexual purity group. Having gone through the hardships of life and come out on the other side, Jason has a heart to see people restored to complete wholeness and freedom, the way God intended them.

For more information, please visit
www.moralrevolution.com
www.ibethel.com

THE 𝒦INGDOM IS COMING LIKE A FLOOD

Heavy Rain
ISBN-13: 978-0-8307-5664-3
ISBN-10: 0-8307-5664-7

In the midst of the darkest epoch season in history, Jesus Christ had the audacity to teach His followers a prayer so shocking that it continues to defy human reason. Jesus turned to His tattered brigade of spiritual warriors and said, "Pray that My Father's kingdom would come and His will would be done on Earth, just as it is in Heaven." Did Jesus intend for His prayer to be prayed by untold billions but to be answered for only a few in some distant eternity? What does The Lord's Prayer have to do with our present-day world, with its mounting crises and its numerous calamaties? *Heavy Rain* unearths the ancient mysteries of The Lord's Prayer to give you answers and prepares the Church for a revolution that will transform every realm of society.

"*Heavy Rain* is sure to play a significant role in releasing the people of God into their glorious role in these glorious days."
BILL JOHNSON, Senior Leader, Bethel Church